W9-CKI-562

90 Days in

John 14–17, Romans, & James

thegoodbook
COMPANY

EXPLORE BY THE BOOK
John 14–17, Romans, & James

© The Good Book Company, 2017

Published by:
The Good Book Company

Tel (US): 866 244 2165
Tel (UK): 0333 123 0880
Email (US): info@thegoodbook.com
Email (UK): info@thegoodbook.co.uk

Websites:

North America: www.thegoodbook.com
UK: www.thegoodbook.co.uk
Australia: www.thegoodbook.com.au
New Zealand: www.thegoodbook.co.nz

Studies in Romans:
Unless indicated, all Scripture references are taken from the HOLY BIBLE,
NEW INTERNATIONAL VERSION. Copyright © 1973, 1978, 1984 International Bible Society.
Used by permission.

Studies in John 14–17 and James:
Unless indicated, all Scripture references are taken from the HOLY BIBLE, NEW INTERNATION-
AL VERSION. Copyright © 2011 Biblica, Inc.™ Used by permission.

ISBN: 9781784981228

Printed in Denmark

Design by André Parker

EXPLORE

BY THE BOOK

90 DAYS IN

John 14–17, Romans, James

with

Timothy Keller & Sam Allberry

Contents

Introduction

"The words of the LORD are flawless, like silver
purified in a crucible, like gold refined seven times."
(Psalm 12 v 6)

This book is not an end in itself. It is a means of accessing the treasures of a far greater book. Its words are valuable only to the extent that they help you to enjoy the infinite value of words that are perfectly true, gloriously beautiful, and utterly wonderful—the words of the LORD.

It is a magnificent thing, in a world which is used to mistakes, to deceit, and to confusion, to be able to read flawless, pure, refined words. And that is what you do each time you open your Bible. God does not make errors in anything he says. He does not obscure the truth, by accident or by design. He does not fail to do anything he has said he will do.

That is why this devotional is an "open Bible devotional"—that is, you will need to keep your Bible open, on your lap or on your screen, as you use these studies. You'll be asked questions that bring you to examine and think hard about the text. The aim of the authors is to cause you to spend more time thinking about God's words than their words.

So, rather than seeing these devotionals as snacks, view them as meals. Set aside half an hour in your day to work through the study, and to respond to what you have seen. They are best done daily—but the most crucial thing is for you to find a pattern that is sustainable—better five studies a week for life, than seven studies a week for only a week!

Further, since every word of the Lord is flawless, we need to read every word in the Scriptures, rather than sticking to our favorite passages, or to an author's favorites. So *Explore by the Book* works, verse by verse, through whole books or large sections of the Bible. You will be moving through both famous books and not-so-popular ones, and within each book through much-used passages and less traveled parts. Expect to discover new favorite passages and memory verses that you had never read or noticed or appreciated before!

At the same time, God's word is not always easy to understand. Whether we are completely new to reading it, or have mined its riches many times, all of us still experience "huh?" moments as we struggle to grasp its meaning! So in this devotional series, some of the greatest Bible teachers in the evangelical world help you to dig up the Bible's treasures, and explain their more opaque aspects. They will show you how what you are reading fits into the great overall story of the Scriptures, and prompt you to apply what you have read to your life.

God's word is not simply pure—it is also purifying. It is the way his Spirit works in his people to challenge and change us. It is designed to move us to worship him with our lips, in our hearts, and through our lives. Each day, you will see one (or both) of these headings: *Apply*, and *Pray*. Use these sections to turn what you have read in God's word into words to speak back to God, and into ways you will change your life in response to God.

At the end of each study you'll find a journaling page, for you to record your response to what you have read, either in words or in drawings. Use these pages as you are led to—we all have different ways of making sure we remember what we have seen in the Scriptures, and of responding to those Scriptures. But here are a couple of very straightforward suggestions that you might like to try:

Before you work through the study, read the passage and record...

The Highlight: the truth about God that has most struck you.

The Query: the questions you have about what you have read (and your best attempt at answering them)

The Change: the major way you feel the Spirit is prompting you to change either your attitudes, or your actions, as a result of what you have read.

After you have done the study, record:

One sentence summing up how God has spoken to you through his word.

A short prayer in response to what you have seen.

I hope you enjoy these 90 days listening to the flawless words of the LORD. Be sure that they will excite, change, challenge and comfort you. Be praying that God would be using his word to bless you. There is literally nothing like the words of the LORD.

Carl Laferton, Editorial Director
The Good Book Company

Note: This devotional is based on the NIV2011 (John 14 – 17, James) and NIV1984 (Romans) Bible translations, but it will also work well with the ESV translation.

Meet the Authors

TIMOTHY KELLER was educated at Gordon-Conwell Theological Seminary and Westminster Theological Seminary, and is Senior Pastor of Redeemer Presbyterian Church in Manhattan, New York City. He is the *New York Times* bestselling author of *the Reason for God*, *The Prodigal God*, and *The Meaning of Marriage*. Dr. Keller is married to Kathy, and they have three children.

SAM ALLBERRY is a pastor based in Maidenhead, UK, a global speaker for Ravi Zacharias Ministries, and an editor for The Gospel Coalition. He is the author of a number of books, including *James For You*, *Why Bother With Church?* and *Is God Anti-Gay?* He is founding editor of *LivingOut.org*, a ministry for those struggling with same-sex attraction.

$$\begin{array}{c} \text{Day} \\ \text{I} \end{array}$$

The Remedy for Troubled Hearts

John 13 v 21 – 14 v 1

John 14 – 17 begins with Jesus telling his disciples not to let their hearts be troubled. His teaching over these chapters is all they need to accomplish this. To set the scene, we need to reach back into chapter 13. Jesus is with his disciples in an upper room. It is the hours before his arrest, and the night before he dies. Jesus has shared a meal with his friends, and he has shocked them by washing their feet, a hugely demeaning act for a teacher to do.

Read John 13 v 21-38

Betrayal

Jesus drops a bombshell. What's about to happen (v 21)? Betrayal by a disciple

He has been hinting at this before (see v 18), but now he is explicit: <u>one of this number</u> will betray him. This sends the disciples into a tailspin, so they nominate someone to ask Jesus who the culprit is.

In verses 26-30, it becomes clear. Judas is the betrayer.

Departure

But then Jesus drops an even greater bombshell...

What does Jesus say is about to happen (v 33)? He is about to leave them.

This is devastating. They have been with Jesus for three years. Some of them have left jobs to follow him. Jesus is their world. He is the figurehead. Without him they are nothing.

Denial

What will happen to Peter (v 37-38)? He will deny Christ

How would this make the disciples feel, do you think? disheartened

Peter, for all his bravado, is going to deny knowing Jesus. Not just once, but repeatedly. This, too, is devastating. Peter has always been the strong one. If he can't pull through for Jesus, what hope do the rest of them have?

Do Not Be Troubled

Read John 14 v 1

This triple-whammy is the backdrop for the start of John 14. We can now see why the hearts of Jesus' friends are deeply troubled. Their world has fallen apart in the space of a few minutes. The Jesus they have come to depend on seems to be abandoning them.

 Have you ever felt as though God had abandoned you?

Many Christians have. There are times when we feel spiritually alone—when God seems very distant and far removed.

What does Jesus tell them to do?

But not just any belief. Specific belief. Belief, or faith, in God. More than that, they are to have faith in Jesus. Belief in God isn't enough. Vague monotheism isn't going to help them. Jesus is. So they, and we, need to listen carefully to all that he's about to say.

⊙ Pray

Ask God to use these devotionals to soothe your anxieties. Pray that God would help you to understand Jesus and to be changed by what he has to say.

~ Notes and Prayers ~
10/24/18

John 14:1 "Don't let your hearts be troubled. Trust in God, and trust also in me."

Lord, tonight seems heavy... in some ways like the disciples may have felt when you spoke of betrayal, departure & denial. Yet, you gave them direction: TRUST! (Believe!)

In God & in you, Jesus. Help me to do that Lord. You are completely trustworthy... despite the darkest night or bleakest circumstances.

"The soul that on Jesus doth lean for repose, I will not, I will not, desert to his foes; That soul, though all hell should endeavor to shake, I'll never, no never, no never forsake."

Day

2

We Will Be with Him

John 14 v 1-4

H ere is a wonderful promise for you to hold on to every day of this life, including today: Jesus gives you the wonderful prospect of joining him as part of his Father's household.

A Home with God

Read John 14 v 1-2

What does Jesus tell us about God's home? More than enough room

"Rooms" can also be translated "abodes." The idea is that there are many places in the Father's house for people to come to and live in. Jesus underlines that this is no trivial point; he has told his followers this deliberately. It is about to have direct relevance for them!

Why does Jesus say he is going there? to prepare a place for them

Jesus is leaving his disciples (which is why their hearts are so troubled in verse 1), but for a positive reason: to prepare a place for them in this wonderful home. He is offering the prospect of them being part of God's immediate family. His going—via his death, resurrection, and ascension—is all for the extraordinary and eternal benefit of his disciples. He is going to procure lodgings for them.

A Home with Jesus

Read John 14 v 3-4

What does Jesus now add to this? He's coming back!

Jesus' going is not permanent. He is going and preparing so that he can return to collect his disciples and personally bring them to the place he has prepared for them.

Why is this such good news? No permanent separation!

Not only does it mean they will see Jesus again, but they will get to be with him forever, living with him in his Father's house. This is comfort for the troubled heart!

⊙ Apply

It is very easy for us to imagine heaven in materialistic terms. We think of all the physical things of this world that we want to enjoy—health, comfort, tranquility, pleasure. We imagine the perfect home in the perfect setting, with nothing to spoil it. But Jesus reminds us that what will ultimately make heaven perfect is being with him and his Father. The Bible does promise us eternity in a new creation (Revelation 21 v 1-4), but what matters most is that we will finally be at home with our Creator. Too often, when our hearts are troubled, we look to many other things to cheer us up. Jesus points us to the full and permanent presence of God that we will one day enjoy. This is where true hope is found.

Has this devotional reshaped your excitement about your eternal future? How?

With whom could you share this comfort for troubled hearts today?

⊙ Pray

"That you may be where I am."

Pray that this prospect of being with Jesus would become what you most long for.

~ Notes and Prayers ~

_____

_____

_____

_____

_____

_____

_____

_____

_____

_____

_____

_____

_____

_____

_____

_____

_____

_____

_____

_____

_____

Day

3

The Way to the Father

John 14 v 5-7

B ecause of the coming of Jesus, no one need ever wonder about how to come to God.

The Way Is Available

Read John 14 v 5

What has Thomas not understood? *where Jesus is going (spiritual)*

Jesus has been teaching throughout John's Gospel that there is a cross awaiting him in Jerusalem. It is the cross by which he will go to the place he has just been describing in verses 1-4. But at least one of the disciples, Thomas, is evidently still thinking in geographical terms. What Jesus is describing doesn't come up on his GPS—so Thomas admits he doesn't know the way. (This may be the only occasion in recorded history when a man admits he needs directions!)

The Way Is a Person

Read John 14 v 6

This is one of the most famous statements Jesus ever made about himself.

How would you put it into your own words?

How does it answer Thomas's question?

Though he hasn't realized it, the "way" Thomas has been asking about is not actually a route, but a person. When it comes to coming to the God of heaven, Jesus does not give advice or directions, but himself. His message is not "Go that way" but "Come to me!" He—not a path or a system—is what we need. Notice too that it is an exclusive claim: only Jesus is these things. What is possible through him is possible nowhere else.

Thomas has been asking about the "way." Why does Jesus add "the truth" and "the life," do you think?

Jesus is not one option among many—a way to find meaning and direction alongside other equally valid options. What Jesus gives us in himself is definitive—*the* truth, *the* life. There is (literally) an eternity of difference between Jesus saying "the" and "a."

But not only that: Jesus is also telling us that he is not just the means to some other end. He is the way, and he is the goal. The life he offers is not life that he has discovered and now has access to; the "life" is Jesus himself.

Read John 14 v 7

What does this verse tell us about the relationship between Jesus and the Father? One

The claim Jesus has made in verse 6 is already enormous, and exclusive. This verse merely brings it to its natural conclusion. The One who is the way, the truth and the life is these things for us because he perfectly expresses who God is. To know Jesus, therefore, is to know the Father himself. There is an implied rebuke here. These disciples have been with Jesus for three years now, and yet they seem to have missed this vital and irrefutable reality, that by knowing Jesus they are not ignorant of who God is and what he's like.

⊙ Pray

These are enormous, life-changing claims, or at least they should be. Pray they would sink deep into your heart and mind.

Think of people you know who need to hear these claims of Jesus. Pray for wisdom to know how to share them, and courage to do so.

⊙ Apply

How do Jesus' claims in these verses comfort troubled hearts? How do they need to affect your heart today?

~ Notes and Prayers ~

" I am... the Life." John 14:6

Jesus is not a pointer to the life
I want. He is not the means to an

abundant life. He is the Life!

Am I using Jesus to obtain the
life (I) desire, or is He himself

the Life I desire?

Lord would you reshape my thoughts
and reorient my desires so
Jesus himself is the Life I
desire and not the means
I use to get to a selfish
man-made ideal.

Day

4

Would You
Like to See God?

John 14 v 8-14

P eople want to see evidence that God is real and at work, but it is not found where you would expect...

The Work of Jesus' Father

Read John 14 v 8-10a

What is Philip asking for (v 8)?

How do we encounter this question today?

Philip is telling Jesus that a demonstration of God would be enough to secure his belief. It is a common way to think. If God were to reveal himself, then that would settle the matter; it is all we need to believe in him. He just needs to show me who he is and that he exists, and that would be enough for me to have faith in him.

How does Jesus respond to this (v 9-10a)?

What is he claiming?

We can almost hear the exasperation in Jesus' voice; showing them the Father is precisely what he has been doing all this time. All he has done and all he has said have been revealing the Father! He is claiming that his words and deeds perfectly reflect the words and deeds of the Father. Though he and the Father are distinct, they indwell each other in perfect unity.

Jesus goes on to say something surprising. "The words I say to you I do not speak on my own authority. Rather, it is the Father, living in me, who..."

How would you expect Jesus to complete that sentence?

Read John 14 v 10b

What does he actually say?

I would expect Jesus to say, *The words I say to you are not my own. Rather, it is the Father, living in me, who is speaking.* But instead Jesus says that as he speaks, the Father is "doing his work." In other words, it is through the words of Jesus that God the Father is working. God works through Jesus' words. This is the answer to Philip's question: to see God at work, all you need is to see what happens through the words of Jesus.

The Work of Jesus' Disciples

Read John 14 v 11-12

What does Jesus promise?

What do you think it means, in the light of what he has been saying?

Jesus can't be saying that we will somehow out-perform him, or have a more powerful or miraculous ministry than him. (It is hard to imagine what that would even look like.) Not even the miracles of the apostles recorded in the book of Acts top what Jesus did.

If it is through Jesus' words that the Father is working, then our "greater works" is not about us doing flashier miracles but multiplying his message. The more his words are shared, the greater is the work done by the Father. In his earthly ministry Jesus could only be in one place at a time. Now, through his disciples, millions of mouths can be speaking his words all over the world at the same time.

⊙ Apply

To believe in God we need to be hearing the words of Jesus. To see God at work we need to be accepting and sharing the words of Jesus.

How will this change your view of reading Scripture? And how will it change your view of your plans and your priorities for your day today?

~ Notes and Prayers ~

Day
5

Introducing...
the Holy Spirit

John 14 v 15-21

J esus is with us, even while he's away from us. We are not left as orphans, to fend for ourselves in this world.

Who the Spirit Is

Read John 14 v 15-17

How does Jesus describe the Holy Spirit?

What is the significance of this?

In many ways, the key word in these verses is "another." The Spirit is to be for the disciples what Jesus himself has already been. He is to be another kind of Jesus, a presence to help the disciples as Jesus has been doing.

The word translated "advocate" means one who gives a legal defense. We should think of him as a (good!) lawyer in a courtroom, whose only aim is to ensure that the truth is heard.

As we have already seen, Jesus himself is "the truth" (v 6). The Holy Spirit is now the Spirit of this same truth (v 17). He has come to bring to the disciples the truth embodied and taught by Jesus.

The Holy Spirit does not have a separate agenda to Jesus. He is the continuation and application of Jesus' ministry.

What the Spirit Brings

Read John 14 v 18-21

What does Jesus mean by saying he will come to his disciples and they will see him, do you think (v 18-19)?

Jesus is not talking about his resurrection or second coming, but the arrival of the Spirit. By the Spirit, Jesus will be with his people; by the Spirit, they will "see" him.

What else will the disciples realize (v 20-21)?

They will come to understand the relationship Jesus has with the Father, and how they have been included in this relationship. The Spirit will make real to them the love that they have in the Father and the Son.

What is the relationship here between love, obedience and the Spirit (v 15-16, 21)?

Love leads to obedience (v 15). Those who love Jesus receive the Spirit (v 16). Obedience to Jesus is evidence of love for him (v 21).

How would you answer the question: Do we have to obey Jesus to be a Christian?

Obedience is not a condition for being a follower of Jesus; but it is a sign that we are one. We don't need to obey Jesus to become a Christian, but we do need to obey him to show that we have become one. If we do obey Jesus (even imperfectly), it is a sign that we love him, which is itself a sign that we are loved by God.

⊙ Pray

Thank God for the gift and work of the Holy Spirit, and pray that the Spirit would help you to obey the words of Jesus today.

~ Notes and Prayers ~

_____
_____
_____
_____
_____
_____
_____
_____
_____
_____
_____
_____
_____
_____
_____
_____
_____
_____
_____
_____
_____
_____
_____

Day

6

Jesus' Plan for World Mission

John 14 v 22-27

Jesus has a plan for how to reach the world with the truth about what he came to achieve. He is ours to embrace, but not ours to hold on to.

Blessing Promised

Read John 14 v 22-24

What seems to be troubling Judas (v 22)?

Jesus has already told us that the world cannot accept the Spirit (v 17), and that the world will not be able to see Jesus but his disciples will be able to (v 19). So the world seems to miss out on all the privileges that are enjoyed by the followers of Jesus.

What does Jesus promise those who love him (v 23-24)?

Jesus repeats what he has already said. Those who come to him, who love him, will find themselves in close relationship with both him and the Father. They will make their home in such disciples. In fact "home" in verse 23 is the same as "room" back in verse 2. We will not be at home with God then unless he is at home with us now. Not loving Jesus excludes someone from all the privileges and promises Jesus has been spelling out.

So far, this doesn't seem to answer Judas' question! If anything, it reinforces it:. Surely such a wonderful blessing can't just be for only a small number to enjoy? We'll get to that!

Truth Promised

Read John 14 v 25-27

What does Jesus promise the apostles?

What confidence does this give us about their teaching in the New Testament?

Some of Jesus' promises are directed to all his followers—to "anyone" (e.g. v 23). But here we have one directed to just his apostles—"to you" (v 26). The work of the Spirit will be to enable these apostles to recall what Jesus has said accurately. It is for those who have been present during Jesus' teaching ministry ("everything I have said to you"). The apostles will be taught all they need by the Spirit. We can therefore have confidence that what these apostles went on to write in the New Testament is reliably God's word. It is what the Spirit taught and helped them to write.

Belief Promised

Read John 14 v 28-31

So... where does that leave the world?

All that Jesus has said about his departure has been to give his disciples advance warning, and to show them why his going is a good thing for them. When it all happens, they will therefore be convinced of his truth. But it will also convince the world of who he is. The prince of this world (the devil) will unwittingly help in all this as he works to have Jesus killed. The message of the cross will enable the world to believe in Jesus.

⊙ Apply

How does this reassure you when the world around you seems so full of unbelief?

You can have confidence that the words of Jesus' apostles will help the world to see the truth of who Jesus is and come to enjoy the blessings of knowing him and his Father.

What part do you have to play in this mission? How will you play it today?

~ Notes and Prayers ~

_____

_____

_____

_____

_____

_____

_____

_____

_____

_____

_____

_____

_____

_____

_____

_____

_____

_____

_____

_____

_____

_____

_____

Day

7

The Divine Gardener

John 15 v 6

As Christians we don't just follow Jesus; we are spiritually connected to him, as a branch is to a tree.

Being a Branch

Read John 15 v 1

Countries often have symbols: the eagle for America, the maple leaf for Canada, and the lion for England. For Israel in the Old Testament era of history, it was the vine. It reminded them that God had planted them in the land to bear fruit as his people.

In light of this, what is Jesus claiming by describing himself here as "the true vine"?

All that Israel were meant to be but never were, he is. Jesus is the one who has perfectly obeyed God before a watching world (see 14 v 31).

If Jesus is the true vine, then the only way we can ever be part of the people of God is by being in him—being included in his righteousness and obedience. Wonderfully, this is precisely what he has come to bring about, promising that we can be in him and he in us (see 14 v 20).

Being Fruitful

Read John 15 v 2-6

What is God's work in the vineyard (v 2, 6)?

The divine gardener is there to cut the branches—to cut off the fruitless ones and to cut back the fruitful ones. We have seen an example of a fruitless branch already: Judas looked to be part of things but was never truly connected to Jesus spiritually (see 13 v 21-30).

Why does he prune the fruitful branches (v 3-4)?

If you've ever pruned a plant, you will know that cutting the branches right back makes them much more fruitful, even if at the time it looks cruel and wasteful. God's purpose is that we bear the fruit of Jesus, manifesting his character and truth (v 16).

Being Pruned

Ultimately, we should be thankful that God is working in us in such a way as to make us more fruitful and like Christ. There will be times when following him becomes very painful. We are to expect this. But we can have the comfort of knowing that God is achieving something wonderful through it, enabling us to bear more and more fruit for Christ.

Being pruned is not pleasant at the time. As with pruning a real tree, it may look harsh and wasteful, and include cutting good things away from us that can be painful to lose. But if it draws us deeper into the life of Jesus, then it is worth it.

What is the alternative to being a fruitful branch (v 2)?

If your life shows fruit—even a tiny amount—then you can enjoy knowing you are "in the vine" (v 4). You have no need to fear the saw; and you can know that the secateurs are used only for your good.

⊙ Apply

How do Jesus' words here re-orient your view of suffering?

Think of a time when you have been pruned (perhaps it is happening right now)? What fruit of love or obedience grew through that pruning? Have you ever given thanks to God that he cares for you enough to prune you?

~ Notes and Prayers ~

_____

_____

_____

_____

_____

_____

_____

_____

_____

_____

_____

_____

_____

_____

_____

_____

_____

_____

_____

_____

_____

_____

A Home for God's Word

John 15 v 7-10

Whatever happens, we need to remain in Jesus. For that to happen, we need to take his word seriously.

Receiving Jesus' Words

Read John 15 v 7-8

What needs to remain in us if we're to remain in Jesus?

Jesus is the truth (14 v 6). His word has already made us clean (15 v 3); it has brought us into relationship with God. That word now needs to be kept in our hearts. "Remain" carries a sense of being at home and settled. Jesus is saying his word needs to find its long-term home in us.

Obeying Jesus' Words

Read John 15 v 9-10

Why should we obey Jesus' commands?

Notice that obedience here is not a condition of receiving Jesus' love; Jesus implies we're already "in" his love. This is how he wants us to stay there.

Loving Jesus' Words

Read Psalm 19 v 7-11

What adjectives are used to describe God's word?

How do these challenge your attitude to God's word?

So often, we see God's word as a chore to read and a burden to obey. But through this psalm, King David challenges us to look at God's word with awe and thankfulness.

What does God's word do for us?

This psalm helps us to see why God's word is so vital. Without it we are foolish and in the dark concerning him and his ways. But with his word we can be wise and joyful. This is why his word is described as being sweet to taste and more valuable than precious metals.

⊙ Apply

We can see why Jesus connects remaining in his love with obeying his commands. Because he is good, all that he calls us to do is an expression of that goodness. So when we walk in obedience before him, it brings his goodness home to us. We see how what he commands us to do reflects his love and care for us. We bask in his love.

Welcoming and retaining God's word means not only regularly studying it, but making sure we take what we learn to heart. Some make the mistake of neglecting to study God's word. Others make the mistake of forgetting to apply God's word to themselves, so that it has no lasting impact. Both are vital. We need to read it, and apply it, with great care.

What implications will this have for how you study God's word?

How does realizing that obedience is a mark and an expression of love for Jesus motivate you toward obedience today?

~ Notes and Prayers ~

_____

_____

_____

_____

_____

_____

_____

_____

_____

_____

_____

_____

_____

_____

_____

_____

_____

_____

_____

_____

_____

_____

_____

Day
9

Ask in My Name

John 14 v 13-14; 15 v 7, 16

Prayer is not about trying to bend God to our will, but about bending ourselves to his.

How much do you tend to pray each day, or each week?

What most excites you about prayer?

What most puts you off?

Virtually every Christian has struggled with prayer. On one hand it is simply speaking to God. It's not complicated. But on the other hand it is a deeply spiritual thing to do; we are coming before our heavenly Father and admitting our need of him. Nothing more obviously cuts against our human pride.

Jesus' Promise

Read John 14 v 13-14; 15 v 7, 16

In each of these verses, Jesus promises that what we ask will be given to us.

What do these verses have in common? How are they different?

In each case it is the disciples who are to do the asking, and to do so in the name of Jesus. In 14 v 13-14, it is Jesus the disciples are to ask, and he will be the one who does it, so that the Father receives glory. In 15 v 7, the asking and receiving is bound up with remaining in Jesus and having his words remain in us. In 15 v 16, it seems to be the product of the fruitful life, and it is the Father who responds to the asking.

Do you think these verses mean anyone can ask for anything and receive it? If you do not, why not?

As we've seen, the promises here are given to genuine disciples of Jesus, who are obeying his word and whom he has chosen to be fruitful. They are not given to just anyone.

In the Bible, God's name is more than a label by which we can address him. It is an expression of who he is—his character and his ways.

So what is the significance of Jesus telling us to ask in his name?

If Jesus' name is an expression of all that he is, then praying in his name doesn't just mean tacking "in Jesus' name" onto the end of each prayer. It means being mindful of his purposes and character as we come to God in prayer. Our prayers are to be shaped and constrained by what we know of Jesus. We are to pray with the grain of his name, and not against it—for the sake of the glory of his name, and not of ours.

Jesus' Priorities

Read Luke 11 v 2-4

In your own words, what does Jesus teach us to pray for?

⊙ Apply

Think about how you might pray the priorities of the Lord's Prayer in your own context this week:

How would you like to see God's name hallowed and his kingdom extended?

Which particular temptations do you need help to resist?

What are your greatest needs as a Christian at the moment?

⊙ Pray

Pray now in Jesus' name, enjoying the privilege, confidence and expectation of doing so.

~ Notes and Prayers ~

_____

_____

_____

_____

_____

_____

_____

_____

_____

_____

_____

_____

_____

_____

_____

_____

_____

_____

_____

_____

_____

How to Show You Follow Jesus

John 13 v 34-35; 15 v 12, 17

J esus' love shows who he really is. That same love among his disciples will show who we really are.

Think of some of the different groups you belong to.

What do these groups mean to you?

Now think about your local Christian community.

What do the Christians there mean to you?

Is this answer the same or different to your previous one?

Read John 13 v 34-35, 15 v 12 and v 17

Why do you think this command is repeated so much?

The Fuel for Our Love

How are we to love one another as God's people? *As he has loved us.* This helps us understand why he describes it as a "new command." God has always commanded his people to love one another, so it's not new in the sense of never having been heard before. No, it comes now with newness because of this unique love of Jesus for us which fuels it. Having been loved by Jesus in this extraordinary, unprecedented way, we are to love one another in the same way. The love we are to show is a love we have already received.

Read John 15 v 13

How is the love of Jesus different than any other kind?

True love is sacrificial, and none has ever been as sacrificial as Christ's. Many in this world have been willing to face death for others. But Jesus has done something even greater. He was willing to bear the spiritual death we deserved—being cut off from the love of the Father.

The Impact of Our Love

Read John 13 v 35

What will us loving one another result in?

Jesus promises that this is the way we will prove to a watching world that we belong to him. The love we share will be undeniably supernatural in origin. There will be no other way of accounting for it other than by the truth of Jesus.

And there will be no limit to its impact. Everyone will be able to deduce this. This promise is good for all contexts and times.

⊙ Apply

Are you in a local church?

If not, consider joining one. We cannot obey this command apart from being in a Christian community.

If you are, think about some of the ways you can apply this command.

What needs are you aware of among your fellow believers?

What could you do to help?

~ Notes and Prayers ~

_____

_____

_____

_____

_____

_____

_____

_____

_____

_____

_____

_____

_____

_____

_____

_____

_____

_____

_____

_____

_____

_____

(Day **11**)

What a Friend We Have in Jesus...

John 15 v 13-15

We all need proper friends in life. And Jesus himself is the truest of all friends.

Read Proverbs 17 v 17; 19 v 4; 27 v 5-6 and 9

What are the marks of a good friend, according to these words of divine wisdom?

Good friends are consistent. They remain friends in good times and bad. They always stick around; they're not just there because you're useful to them. They're also honest. They're prepared to say hard truths, even if it is uncomfortable.

Do you value these traits in friends as much as you should?

Would your friends be able to say them of you?

No Longer Servants

Read John 15 v 14-15

What does Jesus say is the difference between a friend and a servant (v 15)?

How do Jesus' true friends reveal themselves (v 14)?

The servant knows his instructions, but the friend is given the inside track on what is going on. They know all the background. You guard what you say to others, but you're completely open with a friend.

Tim Keller once said that a true friend is someone who "always lets you in and never lets you down." This is why we need friends so much. And it is why we can have no greater friend than Jesus.

What is Jesus' reason for calling us his friends?

Jesus has "let us in." He has passed on to us everything the Father has taught him. That is extraordinary openness!

Read James 2 v 23

How can we become friends with God?

The example of Abraham shows us that believing God—being justified—makes us friends with God.

The Ultimate Friend

Read John 15 v 13

How has Jesus proven his friendship to you?

We see that Jesus is the ultimate friend in a number of ways. He is constant: he will never leave us or forsake us. He is candid: he tells us what we are truly like (and we'll see how he does this through the work of the Holy Spirit in John 16). But his greatest demonstration of friendship is in laying down his life for us. He is the friend who perfectly meets every yardstick for friendship in Proverbs.

⊙ Apply

How will you enjoy the friendship of Jesus this week?

How will you reflect the friendship of Jesus this week?

~ Notes and Prayers ~

_____
_____
_____
_____
_____
_____
_____
_____
_____
_____
_____
_____
_____
_____
_____
_____
_____
_____
_____
_____
_____
_____
_____
_____

If the World
Hates You...

John 15 v 18-25

B eing hated is one of the most awful experiences we can go through in life. But, as Christ's followers in this world, it is an experience we must be prepared for.

Why might the world hate Jesus' disciples?

Not Optional

Read John 15 v 18-19

Jesus tells us that the world hated him. We see that most clearly in the fate that ultimately befell Jesus—death on a cross. But being Christians means that we have now sided with him, and the world has noticed. There are extreme examples of anti-Christian hatred in some parts of the world where societies openly attack Christians, but it is also true (in more muted ways) in the West.

What language does Jesus use to describe our relationship to him and to the world?

We used to belong to the world. The implication is that we now belong to Jesus instead. Following him is about far more than having a vague fondness for him; it is a fundamental shift of our identity and loyalty. Jesus has chosen us to be identified with him. Our relationship to the world has dramatically changed in a way that will provoke deep animosity. It is a necessary cost of the Christian life—not an unfortunate extra for some unlucky followers, to be avoided wherever possible.

Like the Master

Read John 15 v 20-21

What does this hatred of the world reveal?

If I Had Not...

Read John 15 v 22-24

Twice Jesus says "If I had not..."

What has he done, and what has happened as a result?

Jesus is not saying that those who belong to the world were somehow sinless before this. His point is that his coming has made their guilt all the more obvious.

Not the First, nor the Last

Read John 15 v 25

What is the precedent for this (see NIV footnote)?

What Jesus has experienced is both a continuation and intensification of what King David experienced. Our Lord was not the first godly king of Israel to suffer hatred. He was not the last member of God's people to do so.

Jesus knew what was coming, and he was fully prepared for it. It did not take him by surprise, or deflect him from his path of faithful love and obedience. His followers must likewise be prepared, not surprised, and never deflected.

⊙ Apply

Have you thought before about the possibility that you might experience unreasonable hatred from others just for being a Christian? Have you experienced it before?

Think about your character. How would you be most tempted to stray from obedience and love when you experience hatred?

How does this passage help you prepare to be hated, and to walk on through hatred?

~ Notes and Prayers ~

_____

_____

_____

_____

_____

_____

_____

_____

_____

_____

_____

_____

_____

_____

_____

_____

_____

_____

_____

_____

_____

_____

_____

_____

_____

_____

_____

_____

○
Day
13

Forewarned Is Forearmed

John 15 v 26 – 16 v 4

The world may hate God's people, but God's response is to continue to show himself to the world.

A Spirit Who Is Sent

Read John 15 v 26

Look at how Jesus describes the Holy Spirit.

Why is it now important for us to know the Spirit as "the Advocate"?

Jesus has already described the Spirit as "another Advocate" (John 14 v 16), and in the face of this opposition to God's people, we can begin to see why we might need the work of an advocate like this.

What does Jesus tell us about how the Spirit comes to us?

Jesus twice shows us that the Spirit comes from the Father, but also adds that he himself will send the Spirit. The whole Trinity is involved with us receiving the gift of the Spirit!

A Mission to Be Part Of

Read John 15 v 26-27

What will the Spirit do?

The Spirit will testify about Jesus. God will be revealed. But the Spirit is not the only agency by which God will be made known...

What are the apostles to do?

Again, we see something unique to the apostles. They have been with Jesus through the whole span of his ministry. This is an amplification of what we saw in 14 v 26. Through the apostles the Spirit will provide expert testimony about God to the world. The world may have rejected God, but he has not rejected the world. But this doesn't mean it'll be plain sailing for his people...

A Warning to Remember

Read John 16 v 1-4

What else does Jesus tell us about how the world's hatred will be expressed?

Jesus now shows us that there will be religiously motivated opposition, varying from exclusion to the actual killing of some Christians. All will be done in the name of God.

Why is Jesus telling his followers this?

When Christians encounter this hostility, they need not be blindsided by it. If such things happen in our own day (to us or to others we are aware of), we can remember that it is all exactly as Jesus said it would be.

⊙ Apply

God's plan for the world is to reveal himself to it so that more and more people believe in him. We are not to withdraw from the world but to remain in it, and to persevere in bearing witness to Jesus even in the face of opposition, knowing we have been chosen to bear eternal fruit (John 15 v 16).

How will you bear witness today? What might stop you doing so?

⊙ Pray

Pray for your own witness, thanking God that he has called you to follow the Savior who was hated, and to share the news of that Savior even if you are hated.

Pray for the witness of your brothers and sisters who are being severely persecuted around the world right now. Pray for faithfulness, courage, and love—and that determined haters of Christ would become loving subjects of him.

~ Notes and Prayers ~

_____

_____

_____

_____

_____

_____

_____

_____

_____

_____

_____

_____

_____

_____

_____

_____

_____

_____

_____

_____

_____

_____

_____

_____

_____

Day

14

The Prosecution Rests

John 16 v 5-11

I t is going to take something very powerful to convince a spiritually hostile world of the truth of Jesus. And something very powerful is exactly what has been given.

The Gift of the Spirit

Read John 16 v 5-7

Jesus reminds us of what has been going on. He has been preparing his disciples for his departure.

How have the disciples been reacting to this (v 5-6)?

If you think about it, they've been surprisingly incurious about exactly where he's going. Their main focus has been on his leaving them, which has led to their other reaction of grief at the thought of losing him.

Why is it actually better for them that Jesus is going (v 7)?

This takes us to the heart of this whole section of John. The disciples will no longer have Jesus with them, but they will have Jesus in them. This is the promise of his Holy Spirit. By the Spirit they have far more of Jesus than they had previously enjoyed.

It is easy to wish we could have been there to see and hear Jesus first hand. We might imagine faith would have been easier then. But we'd be mistaken! We are actually in a spiritually better position living now than people during the time of Jesus. He shows us why...

The Work of the Spirit

Read John 16 v 8-11

What is the Spirit going to do in the world (v 8)?

What specifically will the Spirit prove to the world (v 9-11)?

⊙ Apply

Why is it better for us to live now, with the gift of the Spirit, than to have been around at the time of Jesus?

How does this increase your gratitude to God for the life and the times he has given you?

⊙ Pray

It is only because of the Spirit doing this convicting work that any of us has come to faith in Christ. Thank God that he showed you the reality of sin, righteousness and judgment.

Pray for two other people who need this same work of the Spirit to happen.

~ Notes and Prayers ~

He Points Us
to Jesus

John 16 v 12-15

Convicting the world of its sin is not the end of the Spirit's work. Through the truth revealed to the apostles he points everyone to Jesus.

More Than You Can Manage

Read John 16 v 12

How do you think the disciples must be feeling by this point?

It is easy to see why all this teaching is so hard for them to take in. Their world has been shattered by the news that Jesus is leaving them. And much of what he's been teaching them will not yet have sunk in.

How the Spirit Will Help

Read John 16 v 13-14

What does Jesus promise them in response (v 13)?

Once again, the Spirit will be the way these disciples come to fully grasp all that Jesus has been saying. Just as in 15 v 27, this promise is directed specifically at these apostles. It is not that the Spirit is going to directly lead each individual believer into all truth, but it does mean we can trust what the apostles have passed on to us in the New Testament as the truth that the Spirit has led them into.

What does Jesus tell us about what the Spirit will say to these apostles (v 13)?

This is truth that the Spirit himself has been given; he has not himself generated it. It is truth that concerns what is going to happen. The Spirit's role is to take what is given from Jesus and to reveal it to the apostles.

What is the purpose of all this (v 14)?

What does this tell us about the relationship between the Spirit and Jesus?

The work of the Spirit it to point people to Christ. As one theologian put it, the Spirit is self-effacing, wanting to direct our gaze and focus onto Jesus. To be Spirit-filled is to be Jesus-centered. The work of the Spirit will always lead to greater love for Christ.

The Trinity at Work

Read John 16 v 15

What else do we learn about the relationships of the Trinity?

Why do you think Jesus is teaching his followers this?

The Father has shared everything with Jesus. And this is what the Spirit has taken and revealed to the apostles. None of Jesus' disciples need worry that the mediating work of the Spirit in any way adds a layer of distance between God's truth and us.

⊙ Pray

Thank God for the work of the Spirit in your life and pray that he might direct you more and more to Jesus.

~ Notes and Prayers ~

_____

_____

_____

_____

_____

_____

_____

_____

_____

_____

_____

_____

_____

_____

_____

_____

_____

_____

_____

_____

_____

Day
16

Back Again, Gone Again, Joy Always

John 16 v 16-24

Jesus has been preparing his disciples for his death and all that will follow from it, so that they know what life will be like following him. Now he gives them a summary outline of what will happen.

Read John 16 v 16

What two events is Jesus describing?

Jesus is going to leave them soon—he will die on a cross. Then after a short period he will appear to them again—he will be raised from the dead. This news—that they will see him again—is new to them...

Confusion Now

Read John 16 v 17-18

How do they respond?

We can appreciate their confusion. They have just come to terms with the fact that Jesus will be leaving them. Now he is saying he will be back with them. It is not clear to them where Jesus' going to the Father fits into all this.

Grief Soon

Read John 16 v 19-22

Jesus recognizes their confusion. But rather than respond with flow charts about how everything is going to happen, he tells them what they're going to experience emotionally.

What will the disciples go through?

Why is childbirth a good parallel?

What causes pain will also bring deep joy. The disciples' grief at losing Jesus will become joy at all that results from his death.

Joy Ultimately

This leaves us with a question. If there joy is in seeing Jesus again at his resurrection, what will happen when he leaves them again at his ascension?

Read 1 Peter 1 v 8

What makes this joy everlasting, even when Jesus is physically absent, do you think?

Jesus says to the disciples that no one will take their joy from them. He must be talking about more than the joy of them being simply reunited with him at his resurrection, for that last for only a temporary forty-day period before his ascension. We are able to experience deep joy during Jesus' physical absence because through the Spirit we enjoy his intimate spiritual presence.

Read John 16 v 23-24

What else is going to change in this time?

The disciples' relationship with God is going to move onto a new footing. Previously they had always needed to go to Jesus with concerns and questions. Now they will be able to go straight to the Father in Jesus' name.

⊙ Apply

What reasons have these verses given you for joy as a Christian?

What can you do to make yourself more mindful of these things?

~ Notes and Prayers ~

_____

_____

_____

_____

_____

_____

_____

_____

_____

_____

_____

_____

_____

_____

_____

_____

_____

_____

_____

_____

_____

Further up and Further In

John 16 v 23-27

We've been seeing the changes that will come as a result of Jesus leaving his disciples. They'll receive the Spirit, and have a new joy. But that's not all...

New Understanding

Read John 16 v 25

How has Jesus been speaking to them up until now?

How is this going to change?

Why do you think he has had to speak in a way that was not literal?

The spiritual realities Jesus is teaching are outside his disciples' frame of reference, so he has needed to resort to figurative speech. But we've already seen why this will soon change. *Read John 16 v 13.* Through the indwelling of the Spirit, the disciples will have personal experience of the Father in a way they hadn't before. Once they know the Father directly for themselves, it will be much easier for Jesus to speak plainly (i.e. literally) of him.

New Access

Read John 16 v 23-24, 26-27

Jesus has already introduced the idea of asking in his name. What does he now add to that idea in these verses?

What potential misunderstanding does he want to avoid?

Coming to the Father in the name of the Son gives Jesus' followers incredible access. We can share in something of Jesus' sonship. But Jesus needs to make a clarification. He's not saying that we offer prayers to him which he then takes to the Father for us, as though he was the Father's secretary.

So why will the Father answer those who come in Jesus' name (v 27)?

It might be hard to take in, but it's there in black and white. Your dealings with him are not procedural. He doesn't attend to your prayers because of some obscure small print he's bound by. Because of your faith in Christ, you're family now. He loves you.

Read John 16 v 28

This is Jesus' executive summary of his whole ministry. He came down from heaven to reveal the Father to us. He will now return to heaven to open the way to the Father.

⊘ Apply

How do these verses underline the privilege and importance of prayer? What difference will they make to your prayers?

⊙ Pray

Thank God for these two results of Jesus' ministry: that through him you can know God the Father, and approach him in prayer.

~ Notes and Prayers ~

_____

_____

_____

_____

_____

_____

_____

_____

_____

_____

_____

_____

_____

_____

_____

_____

_____

_____

_____

_____

_____

_____

Day
18

Progress Report

John 16 v 30-32

Jesus has just explained what's about to change for his disciples. They'll understand the Father and receive his love in a direct way.

Read John 16 v 29

The disciples are already convinced this new understanding has begun. They now get what Jesus is saying.

They're There...

Read John 16 v 30

What have the disciples come to realize?

What in particular seems to have clinched things for them?

This is a significant milestone. They now see that Jesus knows all things—that he has come from God (as Jesus had just told them, v 28). A key sign of this is how Jesus doesn't need to be asked questions.

Read Matthew 12 v 25 and 22 v 18, and Luke 6 v 8

How do these verses illustrate what the disciples have just said about Jesus?

Read Proverbs 15 v 11

What does all this prove about Jesus?

It is God alone who is able to see into our hearts and what we are thinking. Jesus' repeated ability to know the unspoken thoughts of people around him is yet another sign of his being from God. We can hide nothing from him, so he knows what we need to ask even before we've asked it, as the disciples now recognize. Only someone who has come from heaven could do this!

... But Not Quite

Read John 16 v 31-32

How does Jesus evaluate their immediate progress (v 31)?

What is about to happen to the disciples (v 32)?

What events is Jesus referring to?

What does this tell us about their overall progress, despite their recent insights?

It turns out that the disciples are not quite ready to graduate from discipleship school. Their words now are encouraging, but their actions soon will show how fragile their commitment to Jesus really is. Once he is arrested and tried, they will be nowhere to be found. They are not ready to stand with for him. At least not yet...

Humanly, Jesus will be on his own as he heads to that cross... but what about spiritually?

Jesus has not come down to die on his own initiative; he has been sent by the Father and willingly follows his plan.

Read John 14 v 31

What does Jesus want everyone to know about his relationship with the Father?

Jesus is sent, but we mustn't ever think of him as being coerced in any way. He delights in obeying the Father because his will is ultimately the same as his Father's.

⊙ Pray

Thank God for all that Jesus knows about you, and ask that it would draw you closer to him.

Thank God that Jesus was willing to come into this world and to die for you.

~ Notes and Prayers ~

_____

_____

_____

_____

_____

_____

_____

_____

_____

_____

_____

_____

_____

_____

_____

_____

_____

_____

_____

_____

_____

_____

_____

_____

_____

Day

19

Overcoming
the World

John 16 v 33

Jesus concludes this huge block of teaching, and gives us a great reason to take heart!

Read John 14 v 1

What was the situation for the disciples when Jesus started teaching them?

Read John 13 v 33

Why were the disciples so troubled?

When we began these devotionals, we noted that the disciples were troubled in heart because of what Jesus had just announced to them moments before: he would be leaving them. This was devastating; they had given up so much to follow him and could not imagine how they would continue without him.

What is the answer to their troubled hearts (14 v 1)?

Ever since, Jesus has been giving them (and us) reasons to trust him. All that he is about to tell them will show them why he is going, and why it is for their good.

⊙ Apply

Review what we have been looking at through chapters 14 – 16.

What are some of the things Jesus has been saying that you particularly need to trust? How does trusting those things change the way you feel and the way you live?

Peace and Trouble

Read John 16 v 33

Jesus now finishes the block of teaching he began in John 14 v 1.

What does he tell us about the world?

What examples have we already seen of this?

Jesus has been very clear that following in his steps means facing something of what he faced. Because the world hated him, it will also hate his people (15 v 18-19). If that was the end of the story, it would be pretty discouraging. Thankfully, Jesus has more to say.

What reason does he give us to take heart?

What do you think he means by this?

Jesus has just predicted the failure of his disciples to stand with him, and has re-minded us of the ongoing hostility of the world. But this present state of affairs is not going to last.

When a Seed Falls

Read John 12 v 31-33

What is going to happen because of Jesus' death?

How does this show that Jesus has overcome the world?

In his death, Jesus is going to demonstrate his power over the forces of evil. They will nail him to the cross, but he will burst forth from the grave in triumph. If even the most wicked event in human history shows Jesus' ultimate power, what reason do we have for being troubled?

⊘ Apply

Think of the ways in which the world seems to be winning against Jesus. You might think of places where Christianity has been all but eradicated, or of how little regard our cultural elites have for Jesus.

What reason does this passage give for not losing heart? About what circumstance in your life, or nation, or further afield do you most need to remember this?

~ Notes and Prayers ~

_____

_____

_____

_____

_____

_____

_____

_____

_____

_____

_____

_____

_____

_____

_____

_____

_____

_____

_____

_____

_____

_____

_____

Eavesdropping on the Almighty

John 17 v 1-5

The instruction is now finished but we're not done yet. John 17 shows Jesus praying to the Father in the presence of his disciples so that they and we can listen in and learn.

Jesus prays frequently in the Gospel accounts, but this is by far the longest prayer of his that we have. It is amazing to think that the eternal Son is speaking to his eternal Father, and we get to eavesdrop. This will be like no other prayer we've heard.

The Hour Has Come

Read John 17 v 1-2

What does Jesus pray for (v 1)?

Why is this what he prays for at this time?

This is Jesus' greatest longing. This has always been what the Son has desired—that he would bring glory to his Father. But now it is especially crucial. Jesus is about to be handed over, and will soon be crucified. The time has come.

John 17 shows us some of the inner workings of the Trinity. It is like those DVD bonus features that take you behind the scenes and help you appreciate just how much has gone into what you have seen.

How does verse 2 explain what Jesus has just prayed for?

What does this show us about how God is glorified?

Jesus' prayer that the Father be glorified is clearly not some vague, wishy-washy request. Jesus has been specifically given authority to this end. The Father is glorified as people come to Jesus to receive eternal life.

This Is Eternal Life

Read John 17 v 3-5

What is eternal life (v 3)?

How is this different from how we might think of it?

Eternal life is not about finding the elixir of youth, nor about being reunited with loved ones we've lost. Its essence is in knowing both God the Father and his Son, Jesus Christ. This should not surprise us. Jesus has already shown us that he is "the life" (John 14 v 6). He and the Father are the source of all life. We shouldn't expect to find fullness of life other than by being in fellowship with them.

What work is Jesus talking about (v 4)?

In what sense is it at the point of completion?

Jesus is poised to die on a cross for the sins of the world. This will be the means by which people can come into relationship with God.

What is Jesus' priority as he thinks about the death he is about to die (v 5)?

Through Jesus' death the Father will show us the glory of Jesus, as Jesus himself shows us the glory of the Father.

⊙ Pray

Thank God for the eternal life that is found in knowing him.

Pray that your greatest concern in life would be to bring glory to the Father and the Son.

~ Notes and Prayers ~

_____

_____

_____

_____

_____

_____

_____

_____

_____

_____

_____

_____

_____

_____

_____

_____

_____

_____

_____

_____

_____

_____

_____

○
Day
21

Sovereign for His People

John 17 v 6-12

We have had the privilege of listening in as Jesus prays for himself. Now we hear him start to pray for the disciples around him.

Who They Are

Read John 17 v 6-8

How does Jesus describe his disciples (v 6)?

What characterizes them?

What does it mean to be taken out of this world, do you think?

Jesus' description of his apostles is very revealing. There has been a change of ownership. They no longer belong to the mindset of this world. The Father has removed them from the world and given them to Jesus. They have obeyed this call, the gospel summons to leave all to follow Christ.

What can we learn from this description about ourselves?

We'll see in due course that Jesus is praying specifically for his apostles in these verses, but what he has just said of them is true of all his people. We have heard the same gospel call, and now belong to Jesus due to the sovereign work of God.

What do these disciples know (v 7)?

How have they come to know this (v 8)?

We are familiar with the many failings of the disciples in the Gospel accounts, and Jesus himself has reminded them that in just a matter of hours they will all desert him (John 16 v 32). But we mustn't lose sight of what they have understood, even before the work of the Spirit in guiding them into fuller understanding. They have grasped something of the dynamic of the Father and the Son: of how all truth comes to us from the Father and through the Son.

Crucially, they know all this *because of the words Jesus has given them.*

⊙ Apply

What added incentive does this give you to listen to the words of Jesus, both to his apostles and through his apostles?

What They Need

Read John 17 v 9-12

Jesus now turns his attention in this prayer to his disciples.

What does Jesus pray for them (v 9)?

Why do they need this particular prayer (v 11)?

Jesus reminds us of what is about to happen. He is about to leave this world to return to the Father. But because his disciples are remaining, they need the protection of God's power. The goal of this protection is to preserve the unity of these disciples. The oneness Jesus enjoys with the Father is to be a feature of his people too.

In verse 12, Jesus gives the Father something of a status report of God's people.

What's their situation?

We see very clearly the sovereign control of God over all his people, and even over the likes of Judas, who showed himself to be ultimately lost. This may raise some questions, but the big point is the care Jesus has taken.

⊙ Apply

When do you need to know the comforting truth that you are under the protection of God's name?

~ Notes and Prayers ~

Day

22

The Joy of Protection

John 17 v 13-19

As Jesus continues to pray for his disciples, he is clearly very aware that their remaining in this world as his people puts them in a dangerous position.

His Word and This World

Read John 17 v 13-16

Though in the middle of a prayer, Jesus reflects for a moment on why he is praying what he is praying.

Why is Jesus saying these things (v 13)?

Jesus wants nothing more than for his people to share in his joy. This prayer is a means to that end, both in what he is asking of God and the understanding his disciples will gain by listening in.

What is the disciples' present situation (v 14)?

Why is this the case?

Jesus underlines what he has already been teaching. A world that hated him will not feel any differently about his people.

What has been the impact of Jesus giving them his word (v 14)?

Again we see how central and defining the gospel word is to Jesus' disciples. It is receiving this word (from the Father via Jesus) that has set these people apart from the world around them. The gospel is what makes people different and by doing so, provokes the hatred of the world. Yet, paradoxically, it is this same situation in which Jesus anticipates his followers will share his joy.

Having described their situation, in verses 15-16 Jesus now prays directly for his disciples.

What does he pray for?

Why will they need this?

Staying in the world means ongoing exposure to the threat of the devil. As those who now belong to God rather than the world, Jesus' disciples have something of a spiritual target on them.

⊙ Apply

Jesus continues to reiterate how his people are no longer defined by the world around them. God's people are now aliens in this world.

How does this challenge your own view of where you belong?

Do you think non-Christians around you would regard you as being fundamentally different?

Prepared to Be Sent

Read John 17 v 17-19

Jesus has already prayed for their protection.

What does he pray for them next?

Why is this a fitting thing to want for them?

To be sanctified is to be made holy, set apart specially for God. Jesus is praying that God would make these disciples holy. Jesus was set apart for his mission and now his disciples need to be set apart for theirs.

⊙ Pray

Pray, following the example of Jesus, for your own protection and sanctification: that God would spare you from the harm of the devil, and make you more and more holy like Christ.

~ Notes and Prayers ~

I Will Build My Church

John 17 v 20

H aving prayed for himself (v 1-5) and for his immediate disciples (v 6-19), Jesus now turns his sights to the future...

Not for Them Alone

Read John 17 v 20

Jesus has just been praying for the disciples around him at that moment.

Who does he pray for next? And why is that amazing for us today?

Bear in mind, right now Jesus has eleven disciples who are about to desert him.

What is Jesus assuming about the future of his movement?

These eleven shaky disciples will be the start of a much bigger movement. Jesus anticipates many more becoming his followers over time.

Read Matthew 16 v 18

What is Jesus' plan for his church?

How does this fit with what he has just prayed in John 17?

Though there are significant forces arrayed against the people of God, Jesus is intent on continuously adding to his church. We can expect more and more people to become Christians—the very thing he has just assumed in his prayer.

Read Isaiah 9 v 7

What did Isaiah predict about the rule of Jesus?

How is this reflected in the church?

The rule of Jesus on earth will not wax and wane. It will only ever grow. There will be places here and there where the church may decline, but overall it will continue to expand.

The Spirit, the Apostles... and You

Re-read John 17 v 20

How does Jesus say people will become Christians?

What is the role of the apostles?

The disciples will be led into all truth by the Holy Spirit (John 16 v 13); they will then testify (John 15 v 27); and people will believe their testimony about Jesus and turn to him. We have the fruit of the first two in the pages of the New Testament; and we see evidence of the third not only in the New Testament but also in ourselves. If you are a Christian, you are a Christian because you believed in the testimony of the apostles, because you were enabled by the Spirit to believe the truth given to them by the Spirit.

⊙ Apply

What implications does this have for our efforts to share Christ with others?

We cannot hope to lead people to Jesus if we are not also sharing with them the message of the apostles. The latter is what can bring about the former. If we ditch the teaching of the apostles, we will not be able to grow God's kingdom.

How should this passage encourage us in our evangelism?

If Jesus is planning to grow his church, then our efforts to share the gospel are very much going with the grain of his work. It gives us great hope that there is more fruit to come.

~ Notes and Prayers ~

_____

_____

_____

_____

_____

_____

_____

_____

_____

_____

_____

_____

_____

_____

_____

_____

_____

_____

_____

_____

_____

Day
24

That They May Be One

John 17 v 20-23

J esus is praying for all those who will become Christians in the future. Top of his prayer list? Unity.

Unity Matters

Read John 17 v 20-23

Jesus prays his followers would be united.

How important is it to him?

Jesus explicitly prays for this three times, twice asking that his followers "may be one" and then that they "may be brought to complete unity." That he asks for this repeatedly indicates how much it matters to him,

We also need to remember the context for this prayer. Jesus is about to be betrayed, arrested and killed. He is about to face our sin, to go through hell on our behalf. Yet of all the things he could ask for, this is how he repeatedly prays.

What does Jesus tell us about the type of unity he wants his followers to have (v 21)? What is it akin to?

Jesus has a very specific kind of unity in mind. The oneness he prays for is to be like the oneness he and the Father enjoy within the Trinity. Just as the Father and Son are spiritually united, so too should believers be. This is not a unity we can fabricate ourselves; it comes as people joined to Jesus (through the apostles' message) become joined to one another.

Unity Is Ours

Read Galatians 3 v 26-28

How does Paul describe our relationship to Christ?

The language may be different, but the point is clear. Clothed with Christ. Baptized into Christ. All who come to Christ are united to him, "one" with him.

What is our corresponding relationship to one another?

All of us believers, irrespective of our natural human differences, are united. Being one with Christ makes us one with each other.

Read Romans 12 v 5

How does Paul describe the local church?

What is each believer's relationship to it?

We are not just one with other believers in some generalized, universal sense. We express that oneness at a local level as local churches. This is where we see both our union with Jesus and our union with one another worked out.

⊙ Apply

Imagine someone says, "I follow Jesus, but I don't need the church." What do these verses say to that view?

Think about your own local church involvement.

What will it mean for you to live in the light of Jesus' prayer that his followers be one?

~ Notes and Prayers ~

○
Day
25

Maintaining and Attaining

John 17 v 20-23

Jesus has been praying for his people to be one. What should that look like at the ground level? How should we relate to our fellow believers?

Read John 17 v 20-23

What level of unity is Jesus praying that your local church, and every local church, would have?

Often, this unity proves frustratingly elusive, or very brittle.

How unified is your church? And how unified are Christians in your neighborhood?

Unity does not come easily. Let's turn to the letter to the Ephesians to see how churches can attain and maintain (or, in the order Paul talks about them, maintain and attain) the unity that Jesus prayed for and longs for.

Unity Maintained

Read Ephesians 4 v 1-6

Paul is writing to the local church in first-century Ephesus, present-day Turkey. He has just outlined God's great plan of salvation in Christ. Now he calls his readers to live in the light of it.

What does he tell them to do (v 1-2)?

Every application Paul gives us here is relational, and focused primarily on how we relate to our fellow believers at church. We can't live a life worthy of the gospel without relating to other believers.

What does Paul tell us to do about our unity (v 3)?

Interestingly, unity here is not something we construct from scratch. It is some-thing we have already been given and need to maintain. This unity comes through the Spirit of God. It is the answer to Jesus' prayer in John 17 v 21-23. Jesus prayed his people would be one, and they are one. Our job is not to make ourselves one, but to keep ourselves one. So in verses 4-6, Paul stresses the bond of peace by which our Christian unity is protected. This is the fruit of how Paul told us to live in verses 1-2. Living fractiously together contradicts the multi-faceted oneness of the gospel.

Unity Attained

Read Ephesians 4 v 11-13

Paul has just described Jesus' ascension. Now he shows us what this ascended Christ has given the church.

What has Jesus given the church (v 11)?

Paul lists some of the spiritual gifts he describes elsewhere. It is significant that each of those mentioned here involves passing on God's word.

What is the purpose of these particular people (v 12)?

It is the ministry of the word through these offices that will equip the whole church family to serve one another, and build up the church by doing so.

What is the result of all this mutual service (v 13)?

The building up of one another means unity can be reached as believers mature together.

⊙ Apply

Unity is both a given and a goal. It is to be maintained and attained. It is from the Spirit and through the Spirit.

How does this motivate you to pursue and protect unity in your church?

What will doing this mean for you at "ground-level," in practical, relational ways?

~ Notes and Prayers ~

_____

_____

_____

_____

_____

_____

_____

_____

_____

_____

_____

_____

_____

_____

_____

_____

_____

_____

_____

_____

_____

_____

_____

That the World May Know

John 17 v 20-23

The unity Jesus prays for in John 17 is going to be key to reaching the world with the gospel.

The Message of Christian Unity

Read John 17 v 20-23

The unity is among those who have come to believe in Jesus through the message of his apostles. It is not bigger than that or smaller than that. It is not among everyone who thinks they're Christian, or only among every Christian who thinks exactly the way you do!

What is the world going to know as a result of this unity?

We can see now why this unity is so important to Jesus. It is not just for our sake, so that we can enjoy more harmonious time together. It is for the world's sake. A demonstration of this kind of unity will be able to help the world believe...

• that the Father sent Jesus (v 21).

• that the Father has loved his people just as he has loved Jesus (v 23).

The life of God's people can have a huge impact on a watching world. We see this same dynamic in Ephesians.

The Basis of Christian Unity

Read Ephesians 2 v 14-15

Paul is describing how the gospel has impacted both Jews and Gentiles, and transformed their relationship.

What has Jesus done?

How has he done this?

These two intractable foes have, through Jesus, been reconciled. Paul puts this in the strongest possible terms. Jesus has made the two one. His death has done away with the Jewish law that stood like a fault-line between them.

Jesus' purpose in all this is to create a new humanity—a new "man." A new society in him where all the earthly divisions melt away and his people enjoy unity—the very thing he has been praying for in John 17. And again, someone will be watching...

The Wonder of Christian Unity

Read Ephesians 3 v 10-11

The church is this new society created of previously irreconcilable groupings.

What is God displaying through the church?

Who is he displaying it to?

This is heady stuff. It is through the life of his people—even your own fallible church family—that God is showing all of the spiritual powers how unparalleled his wisdom is. This united community, this new humanity, is his trophy, his mic drop to all the forces arrayed in opposition to him.

⊙ Apply

How has all this challenged your view of church unity?

Do you need to think about it differently?

⊙ Pray

Ask God to convict you afresh of the importance of being one with his people.

~ Notes and Prayers ~

What Jesus Wants for You

John 17 v 24-26

J esus concludes his prayer for all who will come to know him. What he wants for us is what we should most want for ourselves.

Think of just three of the most significant things you really want at this time. It may be health, financial security, a particular relationship, or a new job.

How often do you find yourself thinking about these things?

Where You Will Be and What You Will See

Read John 17 v 24

What does Jesus want for you as a believer?

Jesus concludes his prayer with two specific requests. He wants his people to be with him, and for them to see his glory. These are two ways of describing the same thing: seeing Jesus, up close and as he really is.

Read Philippians 1 v 23 and Revelation 22 v 1-4

What will it mean to be with Jesus where he is?

What are the ways in which this might happen?

One day we will be with Christ. If we die, we will go to be with him. But if he returns before then, he will come to establish the heavenly city here on earth, where we will be with him and see his face. Either way, we will get to be with him.

⊙ Apply

This is something Jesus wants for you: for you to be with him.

How much do you want this for yourself? Does your life support your answer, or does it challenge its truth?

Known and Knowing

Read John 17 v 25-26

What does Jesus say his people know (v 25)?

As Christians, we have an inside track on what is going on. We know the Father that Jesus knows. We know this Father has sent his Son into the world. The world itself remains ignorant of this.

Through Jesus we can know God. As we have seen, it is only through Jesus that this can happen. Only the Son can reveal the Father (14 v 6-7).

What does Jesus tell us about knowing the Father (17 v 26)?

Knowing God is not like knowing the rules of chess. It is a life-long process. Jesus has revealed the Father to us and will continue to do so. There will always be more to know.

What is Jesus' aim in this (v 26)?

Christian learning is not like other kinds of learning. It is not ultimately about acquiring knowledge or amassing information. It is about having a greater sense of God's love for us. To know him is to know his love.

⊙ Pray

Pray that you would increasingly want to be with Jesus and to see his glory. Pray that each day from now you would grow in God's love for you.

~ Notes and Prayers ~

You Could Not
Be More Loved

John 17 v 22-26

J esus' prayer in John 17 takes us to the precious heart of the gospel. When
God draws us to himself, he draws us the whole way in.

Think about one of the closest relationships you know about, whether one of your
own or someone else's.

What do you think makes it so close?

Whatever the reason—shared interests, similar outlook on life, a common defining
experience—it provides but a taste of the closeness enjoyed by Jesus and his Father.

The Father and the Son

Read John 3 v 35 and Mark 1 v 11

How does the Father feel about the Son? How publicly does he want this to be known?

Read John 14 v 31

How does the Son feel about the Father? How publicly does he want this to be known?

We are given just a peek behind the scenes at the most precious and exquisite relationship that has ever existed in the universe. The Father and Son delight in each
other and in bringing glory to each other. Each wants everyone else to know how
much they love the other.

Jesus and You

Read John 17 v 22-26

What has Jesus done for us (v 22)?

How does that relate to his relationship with the Father (v 22)?

We are beginning to see that the mutuality enjoyed by the Father and Son is being opened out to us.

We have already thought about the kind of unity Jesus is praying for and something of its impact on the wider world.

What does Jesus want the world to know about God's love (v 23)?

Jesus is saying something extraordinary. Were it not printed in black and white, I would honestly struggle to believe it. He is saying that through him we can be as loved by the Father as he is; that the love the Father has for the Son can be extended to us—that very same love, and not some child-sized version of it.

In verse 26, Jesus makes the same point in a slightly different way. Again, the love of God that we experience and enjoy is the same love that Jesus himself receives from the Father.

⊙ Apply

How should this shape the way you see your relationship to the Father?

How might it fuel your thankfulness to Christ?

When He Had Finished

Now Jesus has finished speaking to and praying for his disciples. It is time to go. *Read John 18 v 1.* It is time to go to the garden where he will be arrested, and to walk toward the cross where he will be crucified. Why? So that his people might enjoy the love that his Father has for him. All that we enjoy in Christ, we enjoy because he died for us.

⊙ Pray

Spend some time thanking God that you—you!—get to share in this incredible love. And spend some time thanking Jesus that he—the Son of God!—went to the cross so that instead of enduring the Father's judgment, you could enjoy that glorious love.

~ Notes and Prayers ~

_____

_____

_____

_____

_____

_____

_____

_____

_____

_____

_____

_____

_____

_____

_____

_____

_____

_____

_____

_____

_____

The Gospel
Dominates

Romans 1 v 1-15

The letter of Romans is all about the gospel: what it is, why we need it, and what difference it makes. The gospel dominates, from the very first verse.

The Writer

Read Romans 1 v 1-7

Who is the letter from (v 1)? To (v 7)?

What is Paul's job, and passion (v 1, 5)?

To be "set apart" is to be separated from other things, to pursue only one thing. The gospel is so great that Paul is willing to separate himself from anything in order to live for it and share it.

The Message

What do we learn about:

• *where we find the gospel (v 2)?*

• *who the gospel is about (v 3-4)?*

• *what the gospel produces (v 5)?*

Paul wants people to obey God—but the obedience he wants is one that springs from faith. What that means is one of the main themes of the letter; but, in short, it is an obedient heart and life that comes from knowing we are accepted and righteous in God's eyes through our faith in his Son, Jesus Christ.

⊙ Apply

The Christian life is not about obeying God *to be* accepted. Nor is it about being accepted and therefore not obeying him. It is about "the obedience that comes from faith."

Do you ever obey because you think you have to, to stay forgiven?

*Do you ever disobey because you know you don't **have** to obey?*

How do you think faith in the Lord Jesus motivates us to want to obey?

The Visit

Read Romans 1 v 8-15

What is Paul's attitude to the Roman Christians (v 8-10a)?

What is striking about this, given that Paul has never met them?

Why does Paul "long to see" this church (v 11-13)?

Paul, the great apostle, does not say in verse 12, *so that you may be encouraged by me*. Rather, he says so that "you and I may be mutually encouraged by each other's faith."

What does this tell us about what all Christians need?

Notice Paul wants to preach the gospel (v 15) to the church in Rome, i.e. to Christians.

What does this tell us about what all Christians need?

⊙ Apply

This week, how can you...

• *allow others' faith to encourage yours?*

• *use your abilities to encourage other Christians?*

• *make sure you are reflecting on the gospel message?*

~ Notes and Prayers ~

Day

30

Eager or Ashamed?

Romans 1 v 16-17

There are two ways to feel about sharing the gospel: eager (v 15), or ashamed (v 16). In these two verses, Paul will help us to be "not ashamed of the gospel."

Before you read on... Why is the gospel shameful, or offensive, to people?

Here are four reasons. The gospel says:

• salvation is undeserved; it offends moral people who think their goodness means they don't need saving.

• we are all sinners; it offends the popular belief in the innate goodness of humanity.

• only Jesus can save; it offends those who think that all spiritual paths lead to the same place.

• the road to glory is one of suffering and sacrifice; it offends those who want following Jesus to be easy and comfortable.

Read Romans 1 v 16-17

I Am *Not* Ashamed

Why is Paul not ashamed of the gospel (v 16)?

What does it do (v 16)? Who for?

This power goes to work in anyone and everyone who "believes." Here we have the first explicit statement in Romans that the only way to receive the gospel and its saving power is through faith. Notice that the gospel does not come with power; it *is* power. It is the power of God in verbal form, and it has the power to change, transform, and give life to people. It does what no other power on earth can do; it saves us.

⊙ Apply

Do you ever doubt or forget the power of the gospel? What causes this?

What difference would it make to you if you had a real grasp on how powerful the gospel is?

What the Gospel Is

What is "revealed" in the gospel (v 17)?

This is a positional word; it means to be in right standing with someone, to not owe them anything. It means to be completely acceptable to someone. So verse 17 is saying that right standing from God can be received from God (chapter 3 will show us how this is possible).

So why is this gospel about far more than simply "being forgiven"?

The gospel is a complete reversal of both the natural tendency of the human heart and the universal thrust of other religions. Everyone else thinks of salvation as being about providing our own righteousness to offer to God. The gospel says salvation is all about receiving a righteousness from God.

⊙ Pray

Thank God for this wonderful gospel. Ask God to make you so excited about what the gospel is, and does, that you are eager about living for it and sharing it.

~ Notes and Prayers ~

Day

31

Why We
Need Saving

Romans 1 v 18-32

Verse 18 literally begins with the word "For." The next chapters will answer the questions: Why do I need saving? Why do I need to receive righteousness from God?

God's Wrath

Read Romans 1 v 18-20

What does verse 18 tell us about God's "wrath," his settled anger?

Why are all people "without excuse" (v 19-20)?

All of Paul's confidence, joy, and passion for the gospel rests on the assumption that all humans are, apart from the gospel, under God's wrath. If you don't understand or believe in the wrath of God, the gospel will not thrill, empower, or move you.

Human Worship

Read Romans 1 v 21-25

What do all people do instead of recognizing God as God, and living in gratitude to him (v 21-23)?

This is counterfeit-god construction. We were created to worship God; so, if we reject him, we will worship something else. Something must give our life purpose and meaning; and we serve that "something." We will either worship the Creator or something he has created. And no created things can satisfy us (because they're not God); and so we find ourselves enslaved by them.

⊙ Apply

Think of an idol you find it easy to worship, serve and obey instead of God.

Why is that thing attractive to you?

Can you identify how it fails to deliver what it promises, and enslaves instead?

Against Nature

Read Romans 1 v 26-32

Verses 26-27 are the longest passage in the Bible specifically about homosexuality. Here, homosexuality is described as "against nature" (*para phusin*). This means it is a violation of the nature God gave us: a sin. But notice that it comes after Paul has identified the root of all sin: worshiping something other than God. And it comes before a long list of other sins, including envy and gossiping. Active homosexuality is no more or less sinful than these—all come from worshiping the created, rather than the Creator.

Do any of the outworkings of "a depraved mind" in verses 29-31 particularly surprise or challenge you?

This whole section is about God's present wrath, which is being revealed (v 18). In other words, God's wrath is simply to "give us over" to the things we worship and want—yet which cannot satisfy or save us.

⊙ Pray

Use this passage to confess to God ways in which you worship created things.

Then use it to prompt you to praise God for who he is, and thank him for his gospel.

~ Notes and Prayers ~

_____

_____

_____

_____

_____

_____

_____

_____

_____

_____

_____

_____

_____

_____

_____

_____

_____

_____

_____

_____

_____

_____

Day
32

The Religious
Problem

Romans 2 v 1-16

S ome people—religious, good people—would read Romans 1 and say, "Yes,
of course God's wrath lies on the immoral. But we're not like that."

Self-Judgment

Read Romans 2 v 1-11

What does Paul say about people who "pass judgment" on someone else (that is, accept that others deserve God's wrath, but don't think that they themselves do)?

The 20th-century theologian Francis Schaeffer called these verses "the invisible tape recorder." It is as though there is a tape recorder around our necks, recording what we say about how others ought to live. At the last day, God will play the tape, judge us on the basis of what our own words say are the standards for human behavior; and no one in history will be able to escape being condemned by their own words.

How is someone who thinks they don't deserve judgment misunderstanding what God is doing (v 4)?

What is this person doing (v 5)?

Why is verse 6 surprising?

Paul is not contradicting 1 v 17, where he said that we must receive righteousness, because we cannot "do" enough to become righteous ourselves. His point here is that on the day of judgment good works are the evidence of our salvation, not the basis of it. Just as the apples on an apple tree prove it's alive, but don't provide life, so the good works we do prove that our faith in Christ has made us alive.

What does Paul add about God's judgment in 2 v 11?

Conscience-Judgment

Read Romans 2 v 12-16

This paragraph is complex! The basic argument is: we are judged by God's law only if we have it (v 12-13); but those without the law sometimes know what is right, and therefore do it (v 14)—showing that the law is intuitively known (v 15). So when someone who hasn't been taught God's law knows what is right, yet doesn't do it, their own thoughts accuse them—they are deserving of judgment.

Chapter 2 is all about Paul showing the Jews (and all religious people) that they have missed the whole point of the gospel. By relying on their own righteousness, they are running from salvation just as much as irreligious people, who rely on satisfying their appetites (1 v 18-32).

⊙ Apply

Paul's challenge is: if you do not feel like a hopeless sinner, whom God would have a perfect right to reject this minute because of the state of your life, you are denying the gospel.

How does this challenge you?

~ Notes and Prayers ~

Day
33

Call Yourself
a Christian?

Romans 2 v 17-29

Remember, in this whole chapter Paul is addressing the religious person, who thinks, "I am not like the pagan. I am moral and religious, so I am not under God's judgment."

Relying on Goodness?

Read Romans 2 v 17-24

What were the Jews of Paul's day proud of (v 17-20—I count six things)?

All this boils down, basically, to a pride in their moral decency and virtue.

What is the challenge to them at the beginning of verse 21?

Paul asks them to consider three ways they may not be practicing what they preach (v 21-23). The third is striking, because there is no record of Jews taking idol-statues from pagan temples. So this is likely figurative; Paul is saying that underneath their outward religiosity, the Jews are worshiping idols just as much as those who go to idol-temples. They may "abhor idols" outwardly, but if inwardly they find meaning in power, comfort, possessions, sex etc., then they are idolaters.

What is the tragic result of this kind of hypocritical religion (v 24)?

Relying on Ceremony?

Read Romans 2 v 25-29

Circumcision was the religious ceremony in which a Jew was brought into the community of Israel.

How much does circumcision matter, does Paul say (v 25-27)?

What "circumcision" matters (v 29)?

No religious ceremony or observance can change the heart. Only the Holy Spirit can do this, and he isn't limited by whether or not someone is circumcised or baptized etc.

Insert "Christian" for "Jew," and "baptism" or "church membership" for "circumcision," and then paraphrase v 17-20 and 25-29.

How does this help us see how these verses might challenge us as professing Christians today?

⊙ Apply

Just because we call ourselves Christians, doesn't mean we have living faith. How can we tell if our faith is empty and we are facing judgment (even if we're an active church member)? Paul alludes to four signs:

1. A theoretical-only approach to the Bible (v 21). We don't allow ourselves to be challenged and changed by it.

2. A feeling of moral superiority (v 17). We look down on others, and are defensive when our weaknesses are exposed.

3. Lack of inner spiritual life (v 29). We don't pray, or know God loves us.

4. Hypocrisy (v 22).

Do any of these particularly challenge you?

⊙ Pray

Re-read verse 29 and ask God's Spirit to work in your heart, increasing—or giving—living faith.

~ Notes and Prayers ~

Day
34

Every Mouth Silenced

Romans 3 v 1-20

Paul now reaches his conclusion. Everyone needs saving—everyone needs to receive God's righteousness—because "there is no-one righteous, not even one" (v 10).

Questions and Answers

Read Romans 3 v 1-8

What is good about being Jewish (v 2)?

The questions of verses 3-8 may not be ones we would naturally think of as we read chapters 1 – 2—they're the objections of first-century Jews. But the fact Paul deals with them shows that he was a man who took time to think about the world-view of those he was speaking to, and who made the effort to deal with objections to the gospel.

No One, No One, No One

Read Romans 3 v 9-18

What is true of everyone—Jew and Gentile, religious and unreligious (v 9)?

This is not to say that everyone is equally sinful. But all are equally condemned, because neither the religious person nor the unreligious person has a righteous heart.

In verses 11-18, how does sin affect our...

- *minds?*

- *motives?*

- *will?*

- *tongues?*

- *relationships?*

- *attitude toward God?*

How can it be true that "no one ... does good" (v 12)? Because the motive matters. If you help an elderly lady across the road (a good act) because you hope she'll give you money (a bad motive), you are not doing good! And if we do good deeds in order to be saved, we are doing good for ourselves, and not for God. It is all selfishly motivated. Good deeds are not done for God—and thus are not truly good—unless a person has accepted and grasped the gospel. But once we know we are loved by God because of Christ, then we are freed to "do good"—to feed the hungry, visit the sick, clothe the poor—and all for their sake and God's sake.

⊘ Apply

How does this idea of "doing good" both challenge you and motivate you?

Every Mouth Silent

Read Romans 3 v 19-20

Why will "every mouth ... be silenced" (v 19) when judgment comes?

What can the law not do? What can it do (v 20)?

A silent mouth is a spiritual condition—the attitude which knows that we cannot save ourselves, has no defense to make, and no goodness to offer. Without a silent mouth, we will never come to God with empty hands to receive the righteousness he offers.

⊘ Apply

Do you, deep down, think that when you stand before God in judgment, you will have something to say? Have you attained the spiritual condition of a silent mouth?

~ Notes and Prayers ~

_____

_____

_____

_____

_____

_____

_____

_____

_____

_____

_____

_____

_____

_____

_____

_____

_____

_____

_____

_____

_____

_____

_____

Day

35

Righteousness Revealed

Romans 3 v 21-26

For two chapters, Paul has been underlining the terrible truth that every human is under judgment. None of us is right with God. "But now..."

Righteousness

Read Romans 3 v 21-26

Righteousness is the crucial word in this passage; and the word "justified" is, in the Greek, the same word. Righteousness is a legal standing of acceptability which is the result of perfect behavior (e.g. to be "right with the law" is to have completely obeyed it, so that it cannot charge you).

What do verses 21-23 tell us about being right with God?

• *Where it comes from*

• *Where it doesn't come from*

• *How it comes to us*

• *Why we need it*

The Just Justifier

But why does righteousness only come through faith in Christ Jesus (v 23); through "faith in his blood," his death (v 25)? Why can't God just forgive people?

The two vital words are "redemption" (v 24—which means to free someone by paying a price), and "sacrifice of atonement," literally "propitiation" (v 25—which means the turning away of someone's anger).

So what did Jesus' death achieve (v 24)?

How (v 25)?

What does the cross demonstrate (v 26)?

How does Paul clarify what he means by this in the rest of verse 26?

This is the wonder of the cross. In the very same stroke it satisfied both the love of God (that wanted to save people) and the justice of God (that demands punishment of sin). God is just—humanity is punished for sin; and God is able to justify (i.e. make righteous) sinners—the perfect man Jesus was punished in our place.

On the cross, both God's wrath and love, both his justice and justifying, are demonstrated, expressed, and vindicated completely.

If our view of God is as a God of love who does not insist on standards and punish wrongdoing, then God becomes uncaring and indifferent (as well as non-existent). We are spiritual orphans. But, on the other hand, a wrathful God without grace makes us feel crushed and despairing, or angry and defiant, never able to live up to his standards.

At the cross, we find that God is a God of wrath and grace. He is a Father worth having, and a Father we can have.

⊗ Pray

Spend some time reading through the verses, using each phrase to meditate on what happened at the cross, and praising God for it.

~ Notes and Prayers ~

_____
_____
_____
_____
_____
_____
_____
_____
_____
_____
_____
_____
_____
_____
_____
_____
_____
_____
_____
_____

Day
36

The Gospel and Boasting

Romans 3 v 27-37

Paul has presented us with a dazzling explanation of the gospel of righteousness-revealed. What lesson does he now draw? "Boasting ... is excluded" (v 27).

No Boasting

Read Romans 3 v 27-30

What you "boast" in is what gives you confidence to go out and face the day. It is the thing of which you say: *I am a somebody because I have that. I can manage what today brings because I am this.* What you boast in is what fundamentally defines you; it is where you draw your identity from.

Why would being saved by "observing the law" (v 27) enable someone to boast?

But we are justified by "faith" (v 27). Why does this exclude all boasting (v 27)?

This is more challenging than it may at first appear. Paul is saying we must give up all our sense of identity and security, all our grounds of dignity and self-worth—because "a man is justified by faith apart from ... the law" (v 28). Whether we are religious (circumcised Jews) or not (uncircumcised Gentiles), there is one God, and one way to be right with him—through faith (v 29-30). To stop boasting is to realize that our best achievements have done nothing to justify us, and that our worst failings do not exclude us.

⊙ Apply

What are the aspects of your life or character that you find easiest to boast about, to rely on, to look to, in which to find your sense of worth ?

How and where do they, or could they, let you down?

How will you replace that boasting with boasting only "in the cross of our Lord Jesus Christ" (Galatians 6 v 14)?

We are not to be self-confident, but Christ-confident. This means we face the day (even the day of our death) saying, *I have Christ. His death means I am God's child. World, I need nothing from you, and you can take nothing from me. I have Christ.*

Uphold the Law

Read Romans 3 v 31

Why might someone think that faith "nullifies" the law?

How does faith in Christ "uphold" the law? First, because it shows the law must be kept in order for someone to be righteous—in Christ's life, it was. Second, it shows that law-breaking will be punished—in Christ's death, it was. Third, it enables us to love the beauty of the law rather than hating it. If we are obeying to be saved, we will either change the law to make keeping it easier, or be crushed by the law because keeping it is impossible.

Only the gospel allows us to care about justice *and* know we are forgiven.

~ Notes and Prayers ~

_____

_____

_____

_____

_____

_____

_____

_____

_____

_____

_____

_____

_____

_____

_____

_____

_____

_____

_____

Day
37

More on Righteousness

Romans 4 v 1-16

P aul now calls two witnesses to support his case: the founder of the Jewish nation, and the greatest king of the Jewish nation.

Read Romans 4 v 1-16

An extremely important word in this section is *logizdomai*, translated "credited" (v 3, 4, 5, 6, 9, 11) and "counted" (v 8). To "credit" something is to confer a status on it that was not there before.

How It Came

What does the Scripture say Abraham "discovered" (v 1) about how to be right with God (v 3)?

How does Paul describe the kind of person whom God makes righteous (v 5)?

This does not mean a saved person does not obey the law, but that they no longer trust in obeying the law ("work") *to be saved*. They transfer their trust from themselves and their efforts to God and his promises.

How is this kind of faith different from "believing in God"?

What did King David discover about being someone to whom God had credited righteousness (v 6-8)?

⊘ Pray

Confess your sins to God openly and honestly, knowing that he forgives them all.

⊘ Apply

It is revealing to ask ourselves, *Why will I get into heaven?* Anything that relies on us, or even our faith (e.g. *Because I am trying to be good* or *Because I believe in God with all my heart*) is not saving faith, because it relies on me.

Abraham would have answered, *Because God has promised to save me, and he keeps his promises.*

How would you answer that question?

When It Came

What question does Paul pose in verse 9?

Why does this matter to us today, if we are not Jewish?

If Abraham was circumcised before he was made righteous, we could say that "faith + circumcision = right with God."

But what is in fact the case (v 9b-11)?

If Abraham obeyed the law before he was made righteous, we could say that "faith + obedience = right with God." But the law was given centuries after Abraham died...

What is in fact the case (v 13)?

⊘ Apply

Why is verse 16 both a good summary of this section, and very exciting for believers today?

~ Notes and Prayers ~

Day
38

Abraham Believed God

Romans 4 v 17-25

What does it mean to believe God? Here, Paul outlines from the life of Abraham what saving faith is.

Read Romans 4 v 17-25

How does Paul describe who God is (v 17)?

And this was the God whom Abraham knew, and trusted, and lived for...

Abraham Believed

What did Abraham do (v 18)?

Why was doing this "against all hope," does verse 19 reveal?

But, despite the apparently impossible nature of the promises, what was Abraham confident about (v 21)?

Abraham did not simply believe God existed, or that he was good and holy. To "believe God" is to look at what God has said and to let that define reality for you. It means:

• *not going on feelings or appearances (v 19).* Abraham looked at his and his wife's bodies, and the idea of having a son was impossible. But he didn't go on appearances, nor trust in himself; he trusted God.

- *focusing on facts about God.* "God had power" (v 21). Abraham knew God had created everything; so he had the power to create life in Sarah's womb. Faith is not the absence of thinking; it is thinking hard about God and what is true about him.

- *trusting the word of God.* "God had power to do what he had promised" (v 21). Believing God is to trust and live by what he has promised—taking him at his word even when feelings, popular opinions or common sense seem to contradict his promise.

And this is the faith that God credits as righteousness (v 22).

We Believe

Abraham is an example to us (v 23-24a).

What "believing" does God credit as righteousness today (v 24b-25)?

Abraham's faith was in God's promise of a descendant; ours is in what God promises one of Abraham's descendants has achieved.

⊘ Apply

How much does the death and resurrection of the Lord Jesus, and the justification it has achieved, define your reality? How could it do so more?

Reflect on your own journey to faith, and your Christian life since then. How have you seen, in your own experience, that God is "the God who gives life to the dead" (v 17)?

⊘ Pray

Thank God that he can do the impossible; that he has justified you; and that he always keeps his promises.

Pray that these truths would define your reality today.

~ Notes and Prayers ~

Day
39

The Joy of Justification

Romans 5 v 1-5

If we are justified, we will one day be in God's eternal kingdom; a wonderful future lies ahead of us. But Paul wants us also to appreciate the benefits justification brings now.

Since We Are Justified

Read Romans 5 v 1-2

It helps to know that "peace with God" is not the same as "peace of God." It is not a feeling, but a state. And "glory of God" refers to his perfect, wonderful presence.

What benefits of being justified does Paul lay out here (try to put them in your own words)?

Without being justified, the opposite of each of these is true of us. How does remembering this help us to appreciate still further the benefits of justification?

But Paul then anticipates an objection: *This is all very well... but right now I am experiencing real pain. What good are these things when I am suffering?*

Even in Suffering

Read Romans 5 v 3-5

What is remarkable about what Paul says about our sufferings (v 3)?

What is it that Christians "know," which means they can view suffering like this (v 3-5)? (Note: It helps to know that "character" means "testedness.")

"Hope" here means a stronger assurance of our peace with God, our access to God, and our future home in glory. The benefits of justification are not only not diminished by suffering—they are enlarged by it.

If I am trying to be justified by works, then suffering will crush me—I will feel that I am being punished for my sins; or it will make me proud—I will think that my suffering means I deserve future blessing. Suffering will drive me away from God, or toward self-reliance.

But if I am justified by faith, then I know that I am at peace with God, that I can speak to him as my Father, and that I will one day see his face. And I know that my suffering has a purpose; that it is detaching me from things I could place my hope in, and encouraging me to place my hope in the only place that can bear my hopes eternally: God himself. Now I can rejoice in my suffering, because my joys remain joys in my sorrow.

⊙ Apply

Think back to a time of suffering in your life (perhaps it is happening right now).

Did that time draw you away from God, or drive you deeper into faith in him?

⊙ Pray

Thank God that, as his child, you can rejoice even as you suffer. Pray that the truth of justification by faith would make this kind of difference to your experience of life.

Speak to God about any areas where you are suffering now, that you would cling on to the truths, and joy, of verses 3-5.

~ Notes and Prayers ~

_____
_____
_____
_____
_____
_____
_____
_____
_____
_____
_____
_____
_____
_____
_____
_____
_____
_____
_____
_____
_____
_____
_____

Day

40

Loved and Assured

Romans 5 v 5-11

How do we know God loves us? How can we really know we will be in eternity with him?

Double Evidence

Read Romans 5 v 5-8

What is the first way in which we know God loves us (v 5)?

This is an internal, subjective ground of assurance of God's love. Paul's language shows that it can be quite a strong experience, though it can also be mild and gentle (which is more common). It is the *experience* of having hope (i.e. certainty) that we are justified in Christ.

How have you experienced this kind of heart-knowledge of God's love?

What is the second way Paul says we know God loves us (v 6)?

People rarely die for those who see themselves as good (v 7a); sometimes people will die for someone who is truly good (v 7b).

But what were we like when Christ died for us (v 8)?

How does the fact that he was the Christ, and we were like this, demonstrate just how much God loves us?

This is objective, concrete evidence of God's love for you. You can look back to a day in history, and point at a man dying on a cross, and know that God loves you.

Our Future

Read Romans 5 v 9-11

What, does Paul remind us, has Christ already done?

What can we therefore be sure Christ will do?

Signs of Rejoicing

What are the signs of rejoicing in your friendship (reconciliation) with God, through the justification Christ has won you? Here are four:

1. Your mind is deeply satisfied with the doctrine of justification by faith. You enjoy thinking and speaking about it.

2. When you discover in yourself a new flaw, the discovery doesn't make you doubt God's love; instead, it makes his grace more precious to you.

3. When you sin, you don't try to excuse your performance, or make up for it. You know your best wouldn't merit acceptance by God, and your worst does not jeopardize it.

4. When you face death, you do so calmly, because you are going to a Friend.

⊙ Pray

Use these four signs of rejoicing to thank God for justifying you; and then pray that your outlook and life would display these signs more and more.

~ Notes and Prayers ~

_____

_____

_____

_____

_____

_____

_____

_____

_____

_____

_____

_____

_____

_____

_____

_____

_____

_____

_____

_____

A Tale of Two Humanities

Romans 5 v 12-21

The previous verses prompt a question: how can one man's sacrifice, as noble as it was, bring about such incredible benefits to so many?

In Adam

Read Romans 5 v 12-14

How did sin and death enter the world (v 12)?

Paul is talking about Adam, the first man.

What does he say happened when Adam sinned in the Garden of Eden (end of v 12)?

The sense of the Greek translated as "because all sinned" shows that Paul is referring to a single, past action. Paul is not simply saying that we all sin like Adam, but that we all sinned in Adam. So, he says in verses 13-14, whether or not people had God's law, everyone died, because everyone was guilty for what Adam did. "Death reigned" (v 14).

Paul is teaching the truth that humanity has a representative—a federal head. Whatever that "head" achieves or loses, we all achieve or lose. One example of a federal head is a president or prime minister. If they declare war, then all their countrymen are at war. If they make peace, then the whole country is at peace. What they do, the nation does.

Before God, Adam is humanity's representative, our federal head. We are dealt with according to what he did. So when he sinned, "death came to all men, because all sinned" (v 12).

In Christ

Read Romans 5 v 15-21

Who is the other federal head introduced in verse 15?

Adam is a "pattern" of Christ, "the one to come" (v 14), in that both are the federal head of a humanity; the merits or otherwise of what they do are transferred to their people.

What does being part of Adam's race bring (v 16-19)?

What does being part of Christ's humanity bring (v 16-19)?

The late John Stott summed it up well: "Whether we are condemned or justified depends on which humanity we belong to ... the old humanity initiated by Adam, or to the new humanity initiated by Christ."

These verses teach us that, if Christ is our representative, whatever is true of him is, in God's sight, true of us.

Think about what Jesus is like; where he is; what he does. In God's eyes, all these things are true of you.

⊙ Pray

Thank God for Jesus' active obedience in his life and death. Thank God that he deals with you through a federal head, so that Christ's life and death are your life and death.

~ Notes and Prayers ~

Union with Christ

Romans 6 v 1-5

Next, Paul deals with some objections to the gospel of righteousness-received, which he poses as four questions. In this study and the next one, we are looking at the first.

The Question

Read Romans 6 v 1

What is the objection?

In one sense, what Paul is about to do is simply to re-explain and re-apply the doctrine of our "union" with Christ—the truth that all that is true of Christ is true of his people—which he outlined in 5 v 12-21. But in another sense, this question introduces a new section of the letter. Chapters 1 – 5 told us what God *has* accomplished for us in the gospel; chapters 6 – 8 tell us what God *will* accomplish in us through the gospel.

The Answer

Read Romans 6 v 2

What has happened to a Christian?

So what should a Christian no longer do?

"Died to sin" does not mean that we no longer can sin, or no longer want to sin (as chapter 7 will show). It means that the moment someone becomes a Christian, they are no longer under the reign, the power and control of sin.

So to "live in it" (i.e. sin) does not mean to sin (otherwise, everyone would "live in it"). It means "to swim in it," to let it be the main driver of your life. So to "live in sin" means to tolerate it, rather than grieve it; and to make no progress with it, rather than to fight it.

The Doctrine

Read Romans 6 v 3-5

What happened when you became a Christian (v 3-4—Paul uses the word "baptized" here to mean conversion)?

What will happen to you because you have been "united with him" (v 5)?

This is a breathtaking outlining of the doctrine of union with Christ. If we trust Jesus, we are "in him"—whatever is true of him is now legally true of us. When he died, we actually died. When he rose, we actually rose.

Why is this the beginning of an answer to the idea: "Christ has saved me, so I can sin more"?

⊙ Apply

Though you may obey sin, and at times you will obey sin, the fact is that you no longer have to obey sin.

How does this both encourage and challenge you?

Is there any area of your life where you are in danger of "living in sin"?

The truth, if you are a Christian, is that you are united with Christ—your sinful old self died with him, and you've been raised to new life with him.

How will this motivate you not to live in the old way any longer?

~ Notes and Prayers ~

_____

_____

_____

_____

_____

_____

_____

_____

_____

_____

_____

_____

_____

_____

_____

_____

_____

_____

_____

_____

_____

_____

Day
43

If We Died
with Christ

Romans 6 v 6-14

In these verses, Paul is continuing to explain our status in Christ, and how that has changed our relationship to sin.

You Died

Read Romans 6 v 6-7

If you are a Christian, what has happened to the old "you" (v 6)?

What is the consequence of this (v 6)?

The "old self" and the "body of sin" are not the same thing. The first is the pre-Christian "me." And so Paul is saying that that person is dead. They died when Jesus died. There is now a completely new "me." But the body of sin still exists, because that is sin expressing itself through our bodies.

So while sin remains in us with a lot of strength, it no longer controls our personalities and lives. That person who could do nothing other than sin has died, and "has been freed from sin." So while we still have bodies which sin, sinful behavior goes against our deepest self-understanding, against our identity.

Imagine a wicked military force had complete control of a country, and a good army invaded and took power and threw the wicked army out of the capital and seat of government. The wicked force was out of power, defeated, but still able to create havoc in the rest of the country, as a guerrilla force. So with the Christian—sin has been thrown out of power, and has no hold over us, yet it still fights hard.

You Live

Read Romans 6 v 8-14

What do we know lies ahead of us, and why (v 8-9)?

Jesus bore and dealt with sin once and for all in his death; his life beyond death is about living for God (v 11).

How should we respond to that truth (v 11)?

What does this mean we must not do; and what does it mean we must do (v 12-13)?

We have "died to sin" (v 2); so why does Paul tell us to "count yourselves dead to sin" (v 11)? Because being dead to sin is like a privilege, or legal right. We have to act on this privilege, and live in light of this truth. Otherwise, we are like someone with financial difficulties who inherits a huge trust fund, but doesn't withdraw any money from it.

It is only as we live as people who are dead to sin and alive to God that we will experience a life free from the power of sin.

⊙ Apply

Where is your fight with sin particularly hard at the moment?

How would remembering what has happened to your old self, and who you are now in Christ, help you next time the battle is raging?

~ Notes and Prayers ~

_____

_____

_____

_____

_____

_____

_____

_____

_____

_____

_____

_____

_____

_____

_____

_____

_____

_____

_____

_____

_____

_____

_____

The Freedom of Slavery

Romans 6 v 15-23

Having died with Christ, a Christian has been "freed from sin" (v 7) and is no longer "under law" (v 14). So aren't we now free to live any way we choose?

Slaves Of...

Read Romans 6 v 15-18

What two things can someone offer themselves to as slaves (v 16)?

How does Paul describe a Christian's conversion in terms of slavery (v 17-18)?

No one is free. Everyone is a slave to something or someone! We all offer ourselves as sacrifices on some altar, serve some cause, and slave for what we see as our highest good in life. What we serve becomes our master; it controls our actions and attitudes.

And Paul says there are fundamentally only two kinds of masters: God (obedience and righteousness) or sin. Whenever we choose not to obey God, we are not choosing to be free; we are choosing to be slaves to sin, rather than our Savior.

⊙ Apply

Is this different to the way you usually think of your choices in life? How?

Think back to last time you chose to disobey God. How were you offering yourself as a slave to sin at that point?

The Two Slaveries

Paul contrasts these two slaveries in terms of their origin, their development, and their results. First, he says "you used to be slaves to sin" (v 17)—this is what we are by nature. It begins automatically; we are born into it. But when "you wholeheartedly obeyed the ... teaching" (v 17—i.e. the gospel), we became slaves of God. This slavery begins when we are converted.

Read Romans 6 v 19-23

What happens as someone lives in slavery to sin (v 19)?

What about as someone lives in slavery to righteousness (v 19)?

As we act in a particular way, with a particular motivation, it shapes our character, and it becomes more natural and obvious to us to act that way again.

What is the result of slavery to sin (v 21, 23)?

Paul is not only talking about eternal future death, but a present death—a "death" people "reap at that time" (v 21). It is a kind of death in life—a brokenness. If we are enslaved to something other than God, we won't reap satisfaction and security, but anxiety, self-pity, a sense of inadequacy, envy, and so on.

What is the result of slavery to God (v 23)?

⊙ Apply

How do you need to apply verse 19 today?

Someone says to you, "I don't want to be a Christian because you have to give up your freedom."

What would you say?

~ Notes and Prayers ~

Not Just Slaves

Romans 7 v 1-6

Paul has been using the imagery of slavery to explain our relationship to God and to sin. Now, he switches the analogy...

Till Death Us Do Part

Read Romans 7 v 1-3

What relationship is Paul now talking about, and what does he say about it (v 2-3)?

What stops a marriage being binding?

Marriage After Death

Read Romans 7 v 4-6

All of us were once "married" to—bound by—the law. It was not a good husband, because we could not satisfy it, and (as we'll see more of in the next studies) the "sinful passions aroused by the law were at work" (v 5). The law brought out the worst in us.

So what did being married to the law result in (end v 5)?

But what has now happened, and how (v 4)?

In Paul's image in verses 2-3, it was the husband's death that freed the wife to remarry. In our case, it is our death in Christ that frees us to "remarry."

Who do we now belong to (v 4)?

What an incredible metaphor—we are married to Christ! To be a Christian is to fall in love with Jesus and to enter into a legal yet personal relationship as comprehensive as marriage. No part of your life goes unaffected.

After all, marriage entails a significant loss of freedom and independence. If you are married, you cannot live as you choose; you have a duty and an obligation. But you also have the possibility of love, intimacy, acceptance and security that you could not have outside marriage. So the loss of freedom in marriage is a joy, not a burden. In a good marriage, your whole life is affected and changed by the wishes and desires of the person you love. You get pleasure from pleasing them. You discover what their wishes are, and then you make changes in order to fulfill those wishes.

So here, Paul gives us the ultimate answer to why Christians obey God. We do it because we are slaves of his, rather than of sin; we also do it because we want to please the One who saved us, to whom we now belong. Obeying the law is a way to please the One we love. So obedience becomes a joy, not a burden.

⊙ Pray

Thank God that he has freed you from slavery and marriage to the law through your death in Christ. Thank God for the new life you now have, with him as your Master and Christ as your Husband.

Speak to God about ways in which you are still living as though sin and the law were in charge of you, and ask for his help to live as the new person you now are.

~ Notes and Prayers ~

Is the
Law Sin?

Romans 7 v 7-12

When we were "married" to the law, our "sinful passions [were] aroused by the law ... so that we bore fruit for death" (v 5). So the law, it seems, is sinful and deadly...

Read Romans 7 v 7-12

When We Read the Law

How does Paul answer the idea that the law itself is sin (v 7)?

What is the purpose of the law (v 7)?

Why is it a good thing that the law does this (think back to 3 v 20-21)?

As we look at the law, it exposes our sin. But that's not all...

As Paul read the command "Do not covet," what did his sinful nature do (v 8)?

Paul is saying that in him—and in each of us—there is a desire to do something for no other reason than because it is forbidden. The law exposes our sin; our sin exploits the law to cause us to sin.

How We See Ourselves

Paul says (v 9) that he was "alive apart from law." He is likely talking about his self-perception before he became a Christian. Because he had never really thought about what the law really required—because he saw it as a behavioral code which he could keep externally—he felt he was spiritually alive, acceptable to God.

But then what happened (v 9)?

Now his self-perception was right—he was dead, a moral failure, unable to save himself. And it was the command not to covet that "killed" him. Coveting is to be discontent with what God has given you and bitter about what he has given others. This command cannot be reduced to an external behavior—it is all about a heart attitude.

So here's what happened to Paul. He read and reflected on this command; and as he did so, his sin prompted him to covet. And he realized that he was not a law-keeper; he was a sinner.

What the Law Is

What does Paul conclude about the law (v 12)?

The law is not sinful—but Paul is, and so are we. Our sin uses the law to prompt us to sin. That's why "the very commandment that was intended to bring life actually [brings] death" (v 10).

⊘ Pray

Thank God for his law, which shows you what is good and godly.

Confess ways in which you have been convicted recently by God's word of your sin.

Ask God to show you ways in which your sinfulness is exploiting your Bible-reading to tempt you to sin.

Thank God that, once you know you are "dead," you can find life through faith in Jesus' obedience on your behalf.

~ Notes and Prayers ~

Day

47

Our Internal Battle

Romans 7 v 13-25

We now come to one of the most remarkable and honest passages in the whole of the Bible.

Read Romans 7 v 13-25

Many thoughtful people have argued Paul must be talking here of his experience as an unbeliever. But it is much more likely he is talking as a Christian. The verbs are present tense; he says: "I delight in God's law" (v 22), which is something only a Christian can do (see 8 v 7); and he knows he is lost but that Jesus will rescue him (7 v 24-25).

Two Pauls

What is Paul like in his "inner being" (v 22)?

But what else is he like (v 23)?

What is the consequence (v 15, 19)?

We all have, in some sense, multiple selves—sometimes we want to be this, sometimes we want to be that. We all face the question: *Which is my true, real self?*

For a Christian, that question is settled, even though the conflict isn't. In our inner selves—in our heart of hearts—we love God, and his law, and desire to live his way. But, as we saw four days ago, there is still a powerful center of sin remaining in us—our "sinful nature" (NIV84), or "flesh" (ESV, NIV2011). Paul says it seeks "what

I hate" (v 15)—and so, he says, "I have the desire to do what is good, but I cannot carry it out" (v 18).

⊙ Apply

Do you recognize this experience of inner struggle in your own Christian life?

How do you deal with it?

Two Cries

What is Paul's conclusion about himself (v 24a)? Why is it accurate?

Why is this cry of despair not the only thing his heart cries out (v 24b-25a)?

These are the two cries of the Christian's heart. Paul is honest about what he is like; but he also remembers what God is like. Christ has rescued Paul from the penalty for sin at the cross, and will one day rescue him from the presence of sin when he returns. *Read Romans 8 v 10-11.*

⊙ Apply

How does knowing that Paul struggled with sin like this comfort you today?

Do you tend to excuse your sin, rather than acknowledge your wretchedness? Or do you tend to forget to look beyond your own failings to Christ's rescue?

⊙ Pray

Heavenly Father, I am wretched. Thank you so, so much for rescuing me through Christ Jesus. Amen.

~ Notes and Prayers ~

_____
_____
_____
_____
_____
_____
_____
_____
_____
_____
_____
_____
_____
_____
_____
_____
_____
_____
_____
_____
_____
_____
_____
_____

Day
48

Right with God

Romans 1 – 7

This devotional is an opportunity to look back over Romans 1 – 7, and enjoy and reflect on the great promises God makes to his people in these wonderful chapters.

For each set of verses, reflect on these questions:

What am I being promised here?

What am I being told here about what it means to be a Christian?

If I believe this more deeply, what about my heart or my life will change?

Space has been left to write down your answers and thoughts.

How Righteousness is Offered

Read Romans 1 v 2-4, 17; 3 v 20-26

_____

_____

_____

_____

_____

_____

_____

_____

_____

_____

How Righteousness Comes

Read Romans 1 v 17; 3 v 22; 4 v 16; 6 v 3-5

_____

_____

_____

_____

_____

_____

_____

_____

_____

_____

_____

_____

_____

How Righteousness Changes Us

Read Romans 5 v 1-5; 6 v 1-2,11-13; 7 v 22-25a

_____

_____

_____

_____

_____

_____

_____

_____

_____

_____

_____

_____

_____

⊙ Apply

In chapter 4, we saw that Abraham discovered that God is "the God who gives life to the dead and calls things that are not as though they were" (4 v 17).

How is this a good summary of all that Paul has told us God has done for us and in us?

How have you seen God doing these things in your life?

⊙ Pray

Thank God for the truths that have particularly struck you and encouraged you from Romans 1 – 7.

Day

49

In Order
That...

Romans 7 v 25b – 8 v 4

W e come now to one of the best-loved chapters in the whole of Scripture...

Through Christ Jesus

Read Romans 7 v 25b – 8 v 2

What does 8 v 1 tell us about being "in Christ"? Why is this wonderful news?

What else has happened to Christians (v 2)?

The phrase Paul uses in verse 1 is much stronger than simply saying we are not con-demned; it is that there is no condemnation at all—no possibility of it. Not only are we not condemned, we can never and will never be condemned.

How does this affect our response to sin?

How does this affect our view of our future?

In chapter 7, Paul showed us that Christians still wrestle with remaining, indwell-ing sin—"what I hate I *do*" (7 v 15). Yet at the same time, Christians now experience a real disgust over sin—"what I *hate* I do."

But there is more to say. Although they sin, for those who are "in Christ Jesus" there "is now no condemnation"—first, not because of their own obedience (chapter 7 has shown that no Christian obeys as they should), but because of the work of God's Son and God's Spirit (8 v 2). And second, because the Spirit now works to do what we cannot—overcome sin. The work of the Spirit is what chapter 8 is about.

His Own Son

Read Romans 8 v 3-4

Why couldn't the law free us from death (v 3)?

How did God achieve it (v 3)?

He did this in order to achieve what?

In his Son, God has defeated the legal penalty of sin—death. But this is not all: through his Son's work, God now sends the Spirit to his people, to wipe out sin in our lives. "The righteous requirement of the law" can now "be fully met in us" (v 4). How can this be? Because we "do not live according to the sinful nature but according to the Spirit."

Verse 4 is telling us that everything Christ did for us—his incarnation, life, death and resurrection—was "in order that" we would live a holy life. Jesus' whole purpose was to make us holy, and able to live holy lives.

This is the greatest possible motive for living a holy life. Whenever we sin, we are endeavoring to frustrate the aim and purpose of the entire ministry of Christ Jesus. If this doesn't work as an incentive for living a holy life, nothing will.

⊙ Apply

In what part of your life do you need to let this truth change you today?

~ Notes and Prayers ~

Day
50

Minding
the Mind

Romans 8 v 5-14

What we dwell on in our minds will shape the way we live our lives. What you set your mind on shapes your character and behavior.

Setting Our Minds

Read Romans 8 v 5-8

What are the two things people can "set" their minds on (v 5)?

To set your mind is more than simply thinking about something. It means to focus intently on something, to be preoccupied with it, to let your attention and imagination be totally captured by something.

Wherever your mind goes most naturally and freely when there is nothing else to distract it—that is what you really live for.

⊙ Apply

What do you do with your solitude?

What does this suggest your mind is set on?

The Realm of the Spirit

Read Romans 8 v 9-14

Who is controlled by the Spirit (v 9, 1st sentence)?

Who has the Spirit (v 9, 2nd sentence)?

What is true of the Christian...

• *now (v 10)?*

• *in the future (v 11)?*

What do Christians therefore have an obligation to do (v 12)?

Christians are not those who live by the sinful nature (or "flesh") and therefore die (v 13); we will, and must be, those who "put to death the misdeeds of the body." Paul is saying that we have been made alive (v 10), and we will one day have renewed bodies (v 11); and for now, we put to death the sinful nature, in the power of the Spirit.

This means a ruthless, full-hearted resistance to sinful practice. "Put to death" is a violent, sweeping phrase—it means to declare war on attitudes and behaviors that are wrong. A Christian doesn't play games with sin—they put it to death.

This also means applying the gospel to our hearts, rather than simply resisting sin in our behavior. We need to remember our obligation to the One who has given us spiritual life now and will give us perfect bodies in the future. Sin can only be cut off at the root if we expose ourselves constantly to the unimaginable love of Christ for us. Sin grows when we think we deserve something from God, or life. Godliness grows when we remember we are debtors to God, throughout life. Putting sin to death is part of what it means to have our "minds set on what the Spirit desires" (v 5).

⊙ Apply

Write down a sin pattern you struggle with.

How can you put it to death?

Think of a "mini-sermon" you can preach to yourself about Christ, and your debt to him.

~ Notes and Prayers ~

Day

51

Adopted Heirs

Romans 8 v 15-17

These few short verses are a wonderful summary of the relationship that you and I, as Christians, enjoy with God, by his Spirit.

Read Romans 8 v 15-17

Children of God

Who are "sons of God" (v 14)?

Verse 15 tells us that this sonship is a "received" status, not a natural one. We are not born as God's children; we are adopted into his family when we receive his Spirit.

In the Roman world, a wealthy, childless man might adopt someone as his heir. (This heir would be male, and so Paul describes all Christians—men and women—as "sons.") The moment adoption occurred...

• the new son's old debts were canceled.

• he got a new name and became heir of all his new father had.

• his new father became liable for all his actions.

• the new son had an obligation to please and honor his father.

Why is it amazing to have been adopted in this way by God?

Privileged Children

What are the privileges of being an adopted son of God?

• *v 15a*

• *end of v 15*

• *v 16*

• *v 17*

In verse 15, Paul draws a distinction between two "spirits"—two ways of thinking about and relating to God. The first is an attitude based on "fear"; the attitude of a slave. A slave obeys because he has to; he fears punishment and is insecure. It is the view that says, "I must perform well in my work for God, and then he will pay me my wages—he will answer my prayers, protect me and so on. But if I perform poorly, he might fire me."

But Paul says we did *not* receive this relationship to God. "You received the Spirit of *sonship.*" The Spirit gives us the ability and confidence to approach God as Father, not as a slavemaster or boss. A child obeys out of love for his daddy; he knows the security of ongoing forgiveness and unconditional love. It is the view that says, "I am a child of God, and he loves me and will give me more than I deserve. My performance doesn't change my position in the family—but I want to work hard for him, because he's my loving Father."

⊙ Pray

One of the privileges of sonship is that the Spirit enables us to "cry, '*Abba,* Father.'" *Abba* means "Daddy."

Pray to God as your Father now. Enjoy this intimacy with him. And cry out to him for help in areas where you are struggling or sad.

~ Notes and Prayers ~

Looking Forward

Romans 8 v 18-27

This world, and each of us, are not what we were meant to be. But one day, we will be. This certainty is what Paul calls "hope."

Read Romans 8 v 18-25

Where Nature Is Heading

What does Paul tell us about nature?

• *v 20*

• *v 22*

The creation is in "bondage to decay" (v 21). It is caught in a continuous cycle of death and decomposition. Life always ends in death.

What does Paul tell us about nature's future (v 21)?

When will this happen (v 19)?

When the full glory of our status as God's children and heirs is revealed, we will bring nature with us. The glory that is coming will be so blindingly powerful that when it falls upon us, it will envelop the whole created order and glorify it along with us.

Some people see the material world as inherently bad—we should withdraw from the world, and be suspicious of physical pleasures. Others see the material world as all there is, and inherently good—we should enjoy, and live for, creature comforts, physical pleasure and beauty.

How does the view of the created world in these verses differ from these views?

What difference will a Christian view of the world make to how we treat it?

Where We Are Heading

What does Paul tell us about believers?

• *v 19*

• *v 21*

• *v 23*

We saw in the devotional on the previous passage how wonderful it is to be Spirit-filled sons of God. Yet all this is only the "firstfruits," a foretaste of the incoming harvest that we will enjoy in the future. We will be completely, totally free from the effects of sin and death in our bodies and spirits.

How do we wait for this day (v 23, 25)?

How the Spirit Helps

Read Romans 8 v 26-27

As we wait, how does the Spirit help us?

How does this encourage us when we suffer, and when we struggle to pray?

When we are too weak to act like children of God, the Spirit helps us.

⊙ Pray

Are there issues in your life that you don't know how to pray for? Bring them before God now, trusting the Spirit to take your thoughts and emotions and to pray on your behalf. Ask for an eager patience about the new creation.

~ Notes and Prayers ~

_____

_____

_____

_____

_____

_____

_____

_____

_____

_____

_____

_____

_____

_____

_____

_____

_____

_____

_____

_____

_____

_____

Day

53

Confident Christianity

Romans 8 v 28-30

Christians can be confident people—but not in ourselves, or in our circumstances. In the last part of chapter eight, Paul shows us the way to deep, unshakable confidence.

Where Confidence Is

Read Romans 8 v 28

What does Paul say "we know" (v 28)?

What people is this answer true for, according to verse 28?

Christians are not shocked by the tragedies and hardness of life—we don't expect things naturally to work for good. When something works out for good, it is all and only because of God's grace, working for us, his children, who love him. When something goes "wrong," we still know with absolute certainty that God is working good for us.

This means we are positive about life, but we're not saccharine or unrealistic about it.

⊙ Apply

How does verse 28 give us confidence in...

• *good times?*

• *bad times?*

• *times of failing?*

How do you particularly need to remember that verse 28 is true today?

How could it cause you to rejoice over an aspect of your life that you would instinctively only grieve or grow anxious about?

What Good Is

Read Romans 8 v 29-30

How do these verses lay out God's ultimate purpose in history?

What do you think each word in verse 30 means?

What is God working to "conform" (or shape) us into (v 29)? How does this tell us what our ultimate "good" (v 28) truly is?

Can you think of a hard time in your life when things went "wrong," but which, as you look back, you can see that God used to make you more like his Son?

Verse 30 is breathtaking. God foreknew his people—before the beginning of time, he knew us in a relational, loving sense. He set our destination, planning for us to be with him in glory. Then, at a particular point in time he called us to have faith in him. As we believed, he justified us—declared and treated us as righteous and blameless. And one day, he will glorify us—make us perfect in body and soul. This lies ahead of us—but because it relies on God's action, not ours, it is so certain that Paul speaks of it in the past tense, as though it has already happened.

⊙ Pray

Use each clause in each verse we've looked at to fuel your thanks to God for what he has done, is doing, and will do, for you.

~ Notes and Prayers ~

_____

_____

_____

_____

_____

_____

_____

_____

_____

_____

_____

_____

_____

_____

_____

_____

_____

_____

_____

_____

If God Is
for Us...

Romans 8 v 31-39

G od is working for his children's good. He has foreknown, predestined, called and justified us, and will glorify us. "What, then, shall we say in response to this?" (v 31).

Four Questions

Read Romans 8 v 31-34

What are the four questions Paul asks here? (Put them in your own words.)

• *v 31b*

• *v 32*

• *v 33*

• *v 34*

What are the answers to each of the questions?

Notice that the answers depend on the truths of verses 28-30.

If the God who has purposed our glory is all-powerful, why be afraid of any opposition?

If the God who has purposed our glory has already given us his most precious possession—his own Son—why worry about our needs?

If the God who has purposed our glory has declared us righteous, and if the Christ who lived perfectly and died sacrificially for us is standing before the Father on our behalf, why listen to anyone (including ourselves) who suggests we are guilty, or unforgiven?

⊘ Apply

Who is opposed to your Christian faith and lifestyle? How does verse 31 give you confidence?

What do you find yourself worrying about? Do you ever worry you won't reach glory? How does verse 32 give you confidence?

What causes you to feel that you are too guilty to be forgiven? How do verses 33-34 give you confidence?

No Separation

Read Romans 8 v 35-39

What final question does Paul ask (v 35a)?

What is his answer (v 37-39)?

All the other questions are really just other versions of this one. The only thing that we really need to fear, the only thing that could really harm us, is to be separated from the love of Christ. And Paul is saying, *Friend, have you been called? Have you found the gospel coming to your soul with power? Have you asked God to justify you? Then realize this—that would not and could not have happened unless the great God of heaven had set his love upon you in eternity before time, and is now unstoppably working out his plan to live with you forever in his family.*

God's love for us does not depend on our attitudes or actions—if it did, we couldn't be certain about life and the future. It rests entirely on his decision and plan. So nothing can separate us from it. We can live with overwhelming assurance.

⊙ Pray

Pray through your answers to the *Apply* section above.

Then spend time thanking God that nothing—nothing—can separate you from his love.

~ Notes and Prayers ~

Day

55

God's Merciful Election

Romans 9 v 1-18

Chapters 9 – 11 are some of the most difficult, and controversial, in the entire Bible. Before we begin, ask God for understanding of his word and humility before his word.

Read Romans 9 v 1-5

How does Paul feel (v 2)? Why (v 3-4a)?

God has done so much for Israel, his people (v 4-5). Yet most of Israel has not put their faith in Christ, and so are not saved. The message should be clearest to them— so why doesn't all Israel believe?

God Chooses

Read Romans 9 v 6-13

What do verses 6b-7a mean, do you think?

Paul turns to two Old Testament examples. Abraham had two children, Ishmael and Isaac; only one was part of God's people (v 7-9). Rebekah (Isaac's wife) had twins, Esau and Jacob; only one was part of God's people (v 10-13). Here, we learn three things:

1. The only difference between Esau and Jacob was God's "purpose in election" (v 11). God chose Jacob, rather than Jacob choosing God.

2. That choice was made prior to birth: "before the twins were born" (v 11).

3. That choice wasn't based on performance—it was made before they had done anything, and not on the basis of any works they would do (v 11-12).

This is the doctrine of election. The only reason Jacob received God's promise—and the only reason anyone has saving faith—is because of God's gracious choice. So, the reason not all Israel is saved is because God has not chosen all Israel to be saved.

Is God Just?

Read Romans 9 v 14-18

What objection does Paul raise (v 14)?

What does salvation depend on (v 15-16)?

Paul's point is that—as God told Moses—God is free to give mercy to whoever he chooses. Mercy can never be an obligation. No one deserves salvation, so God is entirely fair to give it to all, some, or none. God was not unjust in saving Isaac and Jacob.

What did God say to Pharaoh (v 17)?

Pharaoh is a helpful example of how God "hardens whom he wants to harden." In Exodus 4 – 14, God hardened Pharaoh's heart (11 v 9-10). Yet also, Pharaoh hardened his own heart (e.g. 8 v 15). Both are true—God hardened Pharaoh's self-hardened heart. It is what we saw in Romans 1 v 24—God gives people over to what they have chosen. His mercy is never deserved; his hardening is always deserved.

⊙ Apply

How does this passage make you more grateful that you are saved?

Imagine someone says, "God is unfair to save some and not others."

How could you use verses 16-18 to answer them?

~ Notes and Prayers ~

Day
56

Is Election Unfair?

Romans 9 v 19-29

There is a further objection to God's justice in election: if only those God chooses can have faith in him, why are people held responsible for not having faith (v 19)?

Read Romans 9 v 19-29

Have you heard people make the objection of verse 19?

Do you feel it yourself?

Answering Back

In verses 20-21, Paul says that God made us, and therefore he has rights of ownership over us. In one sense, this would be a sufficient answer on its own to the question of "fairness." Who are *we* to answer back to *God*? We are so far below God that we have neither the wisdom nor the right to question our Creator. If you have time, *read Job 38 v 1-41; 42 v 1-6.*

The Heart of the Mystery

What does God "show" in judging those on whom he has not had mercy (v 22)?

What does God "make known," in his mercy and his judgment (v 23)?

In other words, God's glory is seen in him having mercy on some and passing over others. This is the heart of the mystery—we cannot really understand it. Somehow, if God had undeserved mercy on all, or deservedly condemned all, we would not see his glory. The biggest question is: if God could save everyone, why doesn't he? Paul says that God's chosen course (to save some and leave others) will in the end be more fit to show forth God's glory than any other scheme we can imagine.

Further, while God is the author of our salvation, we are the authors of our damnation. The objects of wrath are "prepared for destruction"—but it doesn't say by whom. Romans 1 v 18-24 and Ephesians 2 v 1-3 show that they are prepared for destruction by themselves. Objects of mercy, on the other hand, are prepared for glory by God (end v 23). Salvation, throughout the Old Testament, has always relied on God's undeserved mercy (v 24-29).

⊙ Apply

What difference does the doctrine of election make to us?

1. It prompts us to worship God. I cannot praise myself in any way for my salvation—I will praise God.

2. It makes us humble. It was not our perceptiveness, intelligence or wisdom that caused us to choose God; he chose us regardless of anything in us. There is nothing in us to be proud about.

3. It makes us hopeful in evangelism. Anyone, even the most unlikely, can be saved by God—so I'll share the gospel with everyone I can.

4. It makes us confident. God is in charge of everything, and he is committed to us, to bring us to glory.

Which of these is something you need to ask God to give you more of?

How will you let the truth of election change you?

~ Notes and Prayers ~

Why Israel
Rejected God

Romans 9 v 30 – 10 v 4

Up until 9 v 29, Paul has attributed the unbelief of most Jews to God's sovereign purpose. But now he identifies a different reason for their rejection...

Read Romans 9 v 30 – 10 v 4

A Contradiction?

Through history, the Gentiles "did not pursue righteousness" (9 v 30).

So how have they now obtained this right standing with God (v 30)?

Israel, on the other hand, "pursued a law of righteousness," yet they have "not attained it" (v 31).

Why not (v 32, 10 v 3)?

The Bible is setting two truths alongside one another:

1. God is completely sovereign over all history, including salvation (v 1-29).

2. Every human is completely responsible for his or her behavior (9 v 32 – 10 v 3).

Paul is showing us that God's sovereignty and human responsibility stand in relationship to each other as an antinomy—an apparent contradiction. One example of an antinomy is the fact that light sometimes behaves as particles and at other times as waves—we don't understand fully how that could be (it is an apparent contradiction of physics) but we expect to understand it in the future as we get more information.

What we can say from what God has chosen to reveal to us is that it is God's action alone that saves someone—and that people are lost because of their rejection of the gospel. As the 20th-century pastor David Martyn Lloyd-Jones put it:

"We are responsible for our rejection of the gospel, but we are not responsible for our acceptance of it."

⊙ Pray

Thank God for your righteousness. Every step of your journey to saving faith was under his sovereign control; thank him for them now.

The Problem With Zeal

What is unexpected about the fact that...

• the Gentiles have come to be right with God (9 v 30)?

• Israel has not (v 31)?

What does Paul give Israel credit for in 10 v 2?

So what is the problem (end v 2)?

Zeal must be based on knowledge. Israel's zeal stopped them listening to the gospel; it prevented them from thinking things through.

⊙ Apply

How does verse 2 challenge you? Are you zealous for God? And if you are, is it a reflective zeal or a reactive zeal?

How does verse 2 challenge the idea that "It doesn't matter what you believe as long as you are sincere about your belief"?

~ Notes and Prayers ~

Day
58

What Moses Teaches

Romans 10 v 5-21

To show that Israel were deliberately rejecting the gospel, rather than simply ignorant of it, Paul turns to Moses, through whom God gave his people his law.

What Faith Knows

Read Romans 10 v 5-8

In verse 5, Paul quotes Moses. What does Moses seem to be saying about how to be righteous?

Then Paul quotes from Moses' words in Deuteronomy 30, and makes his own additions (in the brackets). To understand Paul's point in Romans 10, *read Deuteronomy 30 v 1-14*.

Paul says that here Moses is talking about "the righteousness that is by faith" (Romans 10 v 6).

What does Paul say the attitude of faith does not say (v 6-7)?

In other words, faith knows that we don't need to do anything to be righteous. You don't need to scale heaven (Christ has already come down from it), or deal with your own sins in death (Christ has already done that). Faith knows what Moses taught in Deuteronomy 30—that we stray from God and deserve curses and punishment (v 1-2); that God is the one who changes hearts, enables us to love him, and gives us life (v 6); and that this does not require the impossible from us (v 11-14), but simply requires our mouths and our hearts (v 14)...

Read Romans 10 v 9-17

What is all that is required to be saved (v 9)?

What Paul tells us to do with our mouth and our heart are two ways of saying the same thing. Our mouths will profess what we believe in our hearts.

⊘ Apply

Reflect for a moment on your own mouth and heart. Do you:

• *confess that Jesus is Lord?*

• *believe God raised him from the dead?*

If you do, how does verse 9 give you great assurance?

If you do not, will you do so today?

No Excuse

Read Romans 10 v 18-21

Here is Paul's final case against Israel. First, they have heard the gospel (v 18). Second, they have understood the gospel (v 21)—unlike the Gentiles, who have found what they did not seek, Israel have disobeyed what they understood and claimed to desire. Israel are truly without excuse.

⊘ Apply

It would have been easy for Paul to make excuses for his own people's rejection.

Are there people close to you whose unbelief you tend to excuse, instead of sharing the message of Christ with them, and praying for them?

~ Notes and Prayers ~

Day
59

God's Olive Tree

Romans 11 v 1-24

S alvation relies on God's election. Israel was responsible for its rejection of God's gospel. So did this mean that God had utterly, and finally, rejected his ancient people?

Rejection Not Total

Read Romans 11 v 1-10

The question is, "Did God reject his people?" (v 1).

How is Paul himself evidence that the answer is "no"?

Verse 2 reminds us that there are two ways of talking about "God's people." There is the whole of Israel—and then there are those God "foreknew," the elect.

What happened in Elijah's time, when it seemed God was utterly rejected (v 2-5)?

There will always be a faithful remnant within Israel, saved and preserved by God.

Verse 7 is a difficult verse. Remember that Israel sought a righteousness that they themselves could establish (10 v 3-4). So Paul is saying in verse 7 that Israel all sought righteousness, but when confronted with the choice of getting it through works or as a gift, the majority sought it through works, while the remnant received it by faith. And so the majority were hardened; as with Pharaoh, their hearts which were hard to God's grace were hardened by God.

Paul's Hope for Israel

Read Romans 11 v 11-16

How is Paul hoping Israel will respond to Gentiles being saved by the gospel (v 11, 13-14)?

What did the rejection of Israel ("loss") mean for the Gentiles (v 12)?

"Envy" here is not negative. It is not (as it normally is) seeing what God has given to someone else, and wanting it for yourself, though God has not chosen to give it. It is seeing a blessing that God offers to all—salvation—and desiring it for yourself. So, just as the Gentiles could only have heard because Israel largely rejected Christ, so now the Jews can only believe because so many Gentiles have now accepted Christ.

Read Romans 11 v 17-24

Olive trees are cultivated or wild. Paul now pictures Jews and Gentiles as types of tree.

What has happened to the original branches? What about the wild shoots?

⊘ Apply

Paul is "talking to you Gentiles" (v 13)—to us, if we are not Jewish.

How should what has happened to Jews make us feel, and not feel (v 20-21)?

How do we prevent being "cut off" ourselves (v 22)?

If we are chosen by God, we will keep believing and will not be cut off. But we *show* that God's sovereign love is on us by persevering—by remaining grafted into his people.

⊙ Pray

Read Hebrews 3 v 14. Pray that you will continue!

~ Notes and Prayers ~

Day
60

The Future
of Israel

Romans 11 v 22-36

I srael's past is as God's people, to whom he made his promises and to whom
he sent his Messiah, Jesus. But now they have rejected him. What does their
future hold?

A Glorious Future

Read Romans 11 v 22-24

*Given that God has saved "wild branches" (i.e. Gentiles), what can he certainly also do
(v 24)?*

Read Romans 11 v 25-32

What is the "mystery" Paul now reveals (v 25-26a)?

The beginning of v 26 is startling! Who is it speaking of, and what is it saying?

Who? Paul must mean ethnic Israel, all Jews, because this is how he uses the word
"Israel" in verse 25. But "all Israel" probably does not mean every Jew without excep-
tion, but rather, the great mass of Jewish people (especially as in v 32 this is clearly
the way Paul uses "all").

What? They will be saved—which, given Paul's Old Testament quotations in verses
26-27, must mean they will have their sins taken away by a deliverer—by Jesus.

Paul is saying that at some point Israel as a whole will experience salvation through Jesus Christ.

We are not told whether it will happen suddenly or gradually, but we will arrive at a point where more or most Jews have come to believe in Jesus.

⊙ Apply

Do you pray for the salvation of God's ancient people?

Do you know Jews you could seek to share the gospel of the Messiah with?

A Glorious God

Read Romans 11 v 33-36

How are these verses different in tone than the previous three chapters?

What does Paul praise God for?

What do we learn from Paul's worship here?

1. *There should be no worship without truth.* Paul is quoting the Old Testament throughout these verses—Scripture must be the center of all praise.

2. *There should be no study without worship.* Chapters 9 – 11 are dealing with complex, deep doctrines. Paul responds in praise. He uses truth to see and worship God.

3. *Doctrines that exalt God lead to the greatest joy.* The more we see our weak dependence, and God's sovereignty and mercy in election, the more we worship him.

4. *We don't need to understand everything to praise God.* Paul knows he cannot fully trace out God's ways (v 33), but he is not troubled by this. We should praise God for all we know of him, and not be deflected by what we don't understand.

⊙ Pray

Use verses 33-36 to praise God now. Why not begin your prayers for the rest of this month with these wonderful words?

~ Notes and Prayers ~

_____
_____
_____
_____
_____
_____
_____
_____
_____
_____
_____
_____
_____
_____
_____
_____
_____
_____
_____
_____
_____
_____
_____
_____
_____

Day
61

Gospel-Driven Living

Romans 12 v 1-2

Chapter 12 begins, "Therefore." Paul is about to give a summary of the Christian life that should issue from everything he's said about the gospel so far.

Read Romans 12 v 1-2

I Urge You...

What are we urged to do (v 1)?

What do you think this means, practically?

In speaking of sacrifice, Paul uses an image of a worshiper at the temple who comes in with an offering. Not a sin offering (an animal which shed blood for forgiveness)—Jesus is our sin offering. The offering Paul is pointing to is a "whole burnt offering," which was where you brought a valuable, blemish-free animal from your flock. It was a way of showing that all you had was at God's disposal—that you were going to give God your best, not your leftovers.

What is the motivation for living this way (v 1)?

From chapters 1 – 11, what have we seen "God's mercy" is?

The word "spiritual" is better translated "logical." If you have a good view of what God has done for you, worshiping him with everything you have will seem sensible!

Read Romans 3 v 21-26; 5 v 1-4; 7 v 24-25; 8 v 1-3; 8 v 14-17

How do these verses give you a view of God's mercy that motivates you to live sacrificially, out of glad gratitude?

⊙ Apply

To be fully at God's disposal—to offer yourself as a living sacrifice—means:

• actively, to be willing to obey God in anything he says in any area of life.

• passively, to be willing to thank God for anything he sends in any area of life.

How are you currently living as a sacrifice, actively and passively?

In what areas of your life do you need to offer God your best, in a way that costs?

Do Not Be...

What should we not do (v 2)? And do?

Conformity and transformation are not the same things. The first is to be shaped by what is around us. The second is to be changed internally, in a way that also changes us externally.

⊙ Apply

Are there ways you need to:

• *stop conforming to the outlook and expectation of the world?*

• *pray for inner renewal and transformation?*

⊙ Pray

Thank God for his mercy. Use your answers to the apply sections to shape your prayers.

~ Notes and Prayers ~

_____

_____

_____

_____

_____

_____

_____

_____

_____

_____

_____

_____

_____

_____

_____

_____

_____

_____

_____

_____

_____

_____

_____

_____

Thinking about Gifting

Romans 12 v 3-8

Part of being renewed in our minds (12 v 2) is that we're able to see ourselves rightly, and see our place among God's people rightly.

Our View of Self

Read Romans 12 v 3

How should we not think of ourselves?

How should we think of ourselves?

Our biggest danger when it comes to thinking of ourselves is not low self-esteem, but self-centeredness and pride. So Paul tells us to be "sober"—not given to wild confidence or terrible despair like a drunkard, but being rigorously accurate. We're not to think too highly of ourselves; nor too little of our abilities.

Do you naturally think too highly of yourself, or too little?

"In accordance with the measure of faith God has given you" is a strange phrase. Paul probably means: *All of you have been given your saving faith in Christ, and that is how you are to measure yourself.* We are all humbled, and valued, by our knowledge that we are saved through faith alone. The gospel reminds us that we are equal...

Our View of Gifts

... yet we are all different as well.

Read Romans 12 v 4-8

In what way are we distinct from one another as Christians (v 4-6a)?

⊙ Apply

How do you know what your gifts are?

1. Self-examination—take a sober look at yourself. What ministry do you enjoy doing? What problems do you notice and feel burdened by? What are you good at?

2. Ask others whether their opinion matches your attempt at "sober judgment"!

3. Get experience. In general, we don't learn our gifts before doing ministry—we learn them as we minister. So if you think you might be gifted in a certain way, work in that area and let experience guide you.

4. Study the biblical lists. Verses 6-8 are a list of some of the spiritual gifts—others are in 1 Corinthians 12 v 28 and Ephesians 4 v 11. It is hard to discern your gifts without some categories to begin with—which is likely why Paul lists out gifts in these places.

Look through the gifts in Romans 12 v 6-8. (Prophecy here seems to mean preaching, or a message that conforms to Christian doctrine.)

Which ones might describe you?

How are you using those gifts? How could you use them?

⊙ Pray

Thank God for your faith and gifts.

Ask for a right view of yourself, and for opportunities to discern and use those gifts to serve.

~ Notes and Prayers ~

Loving Others

Romans 12 v 9-21

At the heart of the gospel is God's love for us. So at the heart of our lives should be love for him and for others. This short, packed passage shows us how to love others.

Loving Christians

Read Romans 12 v 9-16

"Sincere" (v 9) means unhypocritical—true to our heart. We are not to be polite, helpful, and apparently warm to someone, while disliking them inside. A culture of "niceness" can develop within the church, where a veneer of pleasantness covers over a spirit of backbiting, gossip, and pride.

Why does loving others mean hating what is evil (v 9), do you think?

What happens when we think loving someone means never opposing them?

Real love loves someone enough to be tough with them. If we're not willing to confront someone, we don't love them; we just love them liking us. Real love is prepared to do what is right, even if it risks losing someone's friendship.

Paul could have said in verse 14, *Don't persecute those who persecute you.*

What does he say instead? How is this more challenging?

Loving Enemies

Read Romans 12 v 17-21

The end of verse 20 is an image of someone repenting.

What should we do (v 18, 20)?

What should we not do (v 19)?

All resentment and vengeance is taking on God's role as judge. But only he is the judge; only he knows enough to judge rightly; and Jesus took the judgment of God. Paul is saying, *Either the person you are angry with will repent some day and Jesus will take their judgment; or they will not, and God will deal with it fairly. You are not involved in either process.*

⊙ Apply

Look at the list below and do a personal inventory. Ask yourself:

In which two of these am I weakest?

Where will I need them next (where will I next be tested)?

What practical steps can I take to strengthen myself in these two areas?

• Love people you don't naturally like with sincerity (v 9).

• Be willing to challenge evil (v 9).

• Love with dogged affection over the long haul, no matter what (v 10-12).

• Be generous with your home, money and time (v 13).

• Don't hold on to bitterness or resentment—instead, actively bless those who wrong you (v 14).

• Be willing to be emotionally involved with others (v 15).

• Be humble, willing to associate with people who are different from you (v 16).

• Seek peace in difficult relationships, and avoid revenge if wronged (v 18-21).

~ Notes and Prayers ~

Christians and Rulers

Romans 13 v 1-7

Now Paul moves on to the individual Christian's relationship to the state. This has daily, practical relevance for all of us!

Read Romans 13 v 1-7

The Scope of Obedience

What should every Christian do (v 1, 7)?

What reasons does Paul give?

• v 1

• end v 3

• v 5 (two reasons)

What has God established state authorities to do (v 4)?

Many people obey the state because they don't want to be punished—except when there is no prospect of punishment. But a Christian is to be different—it is a matter not only of fear, but of conscience.

⊙ Apply

Can you think of examples from your life where you can disobey the state's laws without facing punishment?

It is at these moments that we discover whether we are submitting through fear, or due to conscience.

Is there a way you need to stop disobeying and start submitting to the authorities God has established over you? How will you do this?

The Limits to Obedience

Read Daniel 3 v 1-18; Luke 20 v 20-25; Acts 5 v 27-33

How do these passages add to our understanding of how a Christian should relate to the state?

In Romans 13, Paul says that the Christian is required to submit; and he was talking of very non-Christian governments. The default position of the Christian is to obey the government, even when those authorities disobey God's word. Christians are not to undermine a government which *supports* disobedience to God.

But even in these verses, there are hints Paul is not giving an absolute rule—"the authorities are God's servants" (v 6). Obedience to authorities does not trump obedience to God. So it is right to courageously, yet respectfully, disobey and oppose civil authority when it *requires* disobedience to God—as Shadrach, Meshach and Abednego did (Daniel 3 v 1-18), and as the apostles did (Acts 5 v 27-33).

If the state supports what God forbids, we submit. If the state commands what God forbids, or forbids what God commands, then civil disobedience is a Christian duty.

⊙ Pray

Thank God for the authorities he has chosen to set over you.

Pray that you would obey in every way, unless and until you need to disobey in order to obey God.

Pray for Christians in countries who face these complex and costly decisions every day.

~ Notes and Prayers ~

_____

_____

_____

_____

_____

_____

_____

_____

_____

_____

_____

_____

_____

_____

_____

_____

_____

_____

_____

_____

_____

_____

Day
65

Nearer Now
Than It Was

Romans 13 v 8-14

Having detailed our relationship to other Christians, to our enemies, and to the state, Paul now turns to how we live within society, and how we live within history.

The Only Good Debt

Read Romans 13 v 8-10

It is easy to interpret these verses very individualistically. But in verse 7, Paul talks about giving *everyone* what we owe, referring to taxes and honor. Verse 8 is also about paying what we owe everyone; yet now Paul has shifted to the whole body of our neighbors—*all* the citizens we live among. The Bible is clear that while God's people must not become like the world, they are to live in and contribute to the world, rather than withdrawing from it. *Read Jeremiah 29 v 4-7*, a message for God's people living in exile in a pagan city.

What are we to do, and why (Romans 13 v 8)?

What does love not do (v 10)?

In reality, we frequently don't see it this way. In the short run, it often seems that the loving thing to do is to break God's law, not keep it. For example, often we know that telling the truth will hurt someone, so we lie. But Paul says that we are not wiser than God; so keeping his law is always the loving thing to do. Usually, when we talk about doing the "loving thing," we mean "comfortable thing," for the other person and for us.

⊙ Apply

Are there ways in which you need to start doing what God knows is the loving thing, rather than what you think is the loving thing?

The Day That Is Coming

Read Romans 13 v 11-14

If we understand "the present time," what do we know is true (end v 11)?

Because Paul remembers this fact, what does he urge us to do (end v 12)?

What does this mean...

• not doing (v 13)?

• doing (v 14)?

We must behave "as in the daytime." This takes imagination and reflection. We are to imagine that the day has dawned, that final salvation has come, that Jesus is right before us, and ask ourselves, *Now, how would I behave? What is really eternally important? What will last forever?* Or, to put it another way: *Since I am a Christian, legally clothed with Christ, how should I live in a way that reflects my clothing (v 14)?*

⊙ Apply

At what point today do you think you will live differently if you remember "the day is almost here"?

Which desires of the sinful nature do you find it hardest not to think about? How could you think about the Lord Jesus Christ instead at that moment?

How will salvation being a day nearer than yesterday excite you today?

~ Notes and Prayers ~

_____

_____

_____

_____

_____

_____

_____

_____

_____

_____

_____

_____

_____

_____

_____

_____

_____

_____

_____

_____

_____

_____

Day
66

Disputable Judgments

Romans 14 v 1-23

Chapters 1 – 5 of Romans enable us to understand the gospel... chapters 6 – 8, to experience it... chapters 12 – 13, to live it out lovingly. In chapter 14, Paul applies it to a specific issue.

Read Romans 14 v 1-23

The Basic Principle

What is the principle (v 1)?

What "disputable matters" seem to have been causing problems within this congregation?

• v 2-3

• v 5

• v 21

A Christian "whose faith is weak" (v 1) is not someone who is struggling with doubts. It is someone who loses the focus of the gospel—that we are not accepted by God because we keep to a list of do's and dont's, but because we are in Christ. They may believe in Christ very strongly, and be fervent about pleasing him. But they are weaker in that they haven't applied the gospel of justification by grace alone to various areas of their lives.

A stronger Christian in this sense is simply one who knows that they are free to choose how to live and worship in particular areas—for instance, in drinking alcohol, or what style of music to use in church.

Why should stronger and weaker Christians not condemn each other?

• *end v 3-4*

• *v 9-10*

A Word to the Weak

Verse 3 reminds the "weak" that they will tend to judge—to condemn—the "strong." They will tend to denounce the strong as doing things which are displeasing to God, without pausing to consider whether this might be an area of life where Christians are free to live as they choose.

So Paul has two words for the "weak."

First... In Rome, the weaker Christians thought eating meat was wrong.

What does Paul say to that (v 14a)? What is he saying about the weak Christians' opinion?

Paul is bluntly saying that their position is not biblical! When we are tempted to condemn another Christian as "wrong," we need to first ask: "What does the Bible say? Could it be that I am wrong, not them?"

Second... What are we not to "pass judgment" about (v 1)?

Weak Christians need to learn to distinguish between matters of principle (i.e. where God has expressly forbidden or commanded something) and matters of individual preference, or of broad disagreement between Christians. We need to ask, "Does the Bible give freedom on this issue? Could it be that I am making a disputable matter into an indisputable one?"

⊘ Apply

What are the "disputable matters" among Christians in your church or culture, which see Christians condemning others (remember that not every matter is disputable!)?

~ Notes and Prayers ~

Day
67

A Word to the Strong

Romans 14 v 1-23

We've seen Paul challenging the weak Christian; the stronger Christian's position is more biblical (v 14). But then he gives more criticism to the strong than the weak!

Read Romans 14 v 1-23

In the Right...

Remember, a "strong" Christian is one who has a grasp on the gospel—who knows that we are acceptable to God in Christ, not because we keep rules; and who understands the difference between matters of biblical command, and matters of conscience—"disputable matters" (v 1).

How does this Christian, who "eats everything," tend to look at their weaker brothers and sisters (v 3)?

Since their practice is not forbidden by God, why should they stop doing it?! It's the weaker Christian's problem, not theirs—they are in the right, and are clearly wiser and more mature than the weaker Christians who have the issue.

But Be Very Careful...

What is the stronger Christian's problem (v 15)?

How is the end of verse 15 a stark warning to stronger Christians?

If a strong Christian's behavior leads a weak Christian to follow their example, against their conscience, then the weak Christian is sinning (v 23)—they prioritize fitting in, or their own enjoyment, over faithfulness to God. And they will feel guilty, and then ignore that guilt, and become open to doing other things that are truly wrong. So the stronger Christian, even though their actions are permitted, has "destroyed" the weaker Christian. And, Paul adds, Christ died for them (v 15). He treated them with utmost care, and so must other Christians.

What point is Paul making in v 17-18? What should be the priority in how we choose to live as Christians?

Why would verse 20 be a helpful corrective to a Christian who is tempted to continue behaving in a way another Christian finds wrong or troubling?

⊙ Apply

Do you ever think about how your (right) behavior might impact on other Christians?

Are there things that you could, and should, stop doing, in order to help and encourage weaker believers? Are you willing to curb your freedom for the sake of others?

Are there things you condemn other Christians for that are really matters of conscience, and disputable?

⊙ Pray

It takes great wisdom to see where we are being weak and/or strong.

Pray that God would enable you to see any areas where you are being weak and condemnatory, or strong but acting as a stumbling block. Talk to the Lord about any specific ways Paul's words have challenged you.

~ Notes and Prayers ~

_____
_____
_____
_____
_____
_____
_____
_____
_____
_____
_____
_____
_____
_____
_____
_____
_____
_____
_____
_____
_____
_____
_____

Day
(68)

A Life
of Unity

Romans 15 v 1-13

In his final two chapters, Paul continues to apply the gospel to the church,
focusing on unity and mission.

Living for Others

Read Romans 15 v 1-4

What two principles does Paul lay down here?

• *v 1*

• *v 2*

This is about our "neighbor" (v 2)—not only our Christian family, but everyone.

Whose example are we following when we live like this (v 3)?

Paul makes this point with an Old Testament quotation, which leads him to make a
brief, significant comment about the Bible.

Why was every part of the Scriptures written (v 4)?

This means the Bible is: entirely applicable to today—every bit is designed for us,
and has lessons and applications for us; it is centered on Christ (Paul quotes from
Psalm 69 and applies it to Christ, because all the Scriptures are about him—see Luke

24 v 27); and hope-increasing—as we listen to the Bible, we find ourselves enduring in hard work and discipline, and encouraged by its precious promises.

⊙ Apply

The sweeping principle for Christian living here is that wherever we have power (whether it is financial, or social, or in terms of popularity or confidence), we must use that power to build up and do good for those who do not have it.

How would this apply to our:

• *finances?*

• *church leadership?*

• *relationships?*

• *choice of where to live?*

How are you currently obeying verse 2?

How could you do so in new or increased ways?

How will you use verse 3 to motivate you?

Living with Others

Read Romans 15 v 5-13

What does Paul pray this church will be given (v 5)?

How do we live out this "unity" (v 7)?

We learn here that real Christian unity:

• is a supernatural gift—no method can create it, we need God to give it.

• comes from discipleship—unity is a by-product of seeking something other than unity, i.e. following Christ (v 5). Unity doesn't come by seeking it directly.

• happens as we worship together—"one ... mouth" (v 6) likely means corporate worship.

• is based on justification by Christ (v 7)—as we realize God accepts us despite our flaws, we accept others in the same way.

• is part of God's great plan—both Jews and Gentiles are brought together by the gospel to praise God (v 8-12).

~ Notes and Prayers ~

Day
69

A Life on Mission

Romans 15 v 14-24

Paul spent his life, and gave his life, sharing the gospel with thousands of people. Why? And how? And how can his example help us in our evangelism today?

Read Romans 15 v 14-24

Paul's Motive

What is the motive behind Paul's evangelism (v 16-17)?

He describes evangelism as a "priestly duty" (v 16). The Old Testament duty of a priest was to offer sacrifices; so Paul is saying that his evangelism is part of the way he offers himself as a living sacrifice (see Romans 12 v 1). It is a way he can give God praise and thanks—an offering in response to all Jesus has given him.

Paul's Purpose

What is the purpose of Paul's evangelism (v 18)?

So Paul returns to where he started—his mission to call the Gentiles to "the obedience that comes from faith" (1 v 5). Paul is not looking for some kind of conversion experience, but for completely changed lives.

Paul's Means

What is the means of Paul's evangelism (end v 18)?

We are not only to tell people the gospel, but to embody it in our attitudes and relationships. We are to invite people to look into us deeply and see what a human life looks like when rearranged by the gospel.

Paul mentions "the power of signs and miracles" (v 19) that accompanied his message. *Read 2 Corinthians 12 v 12*, where Paul comments that these are "the things that mark an apostle." So it appears that, while miracles can of course happen today, we should not expect (or demand) them. Our "works" will likely not be powerful miracles—they will be the amazing witness of changed, obedient lives.

Paul's Strategy

Lastly, we see the strategy behind Paul's evangelism. He was a pioneer, preaching "where Christ was not known" (Romans 15 v 20). And he was urban—following Paul's journeys from Jerusalem to Illyricum (v 19) shows that he preached and planted in cities, and then moved on, leaving others to take the message to the surrounding areas.

⊙ Apply

Paul had special gifts as an apostle-evangelist—the power of signs and miracles—that we don't share. And he had a particular calling—to pioneer urban church-planting—which we may or may not share. But we can still learn much from his example...

Are you motivated to share the gospel with people? Who will you try to share the gospel of Jesus with this week?

When talking about Jesus, do you make it clear that conversion means a complete life change? If not, why do you think you leave it out?

How are your works matching your words? Does anything need to change?

~ Notes and Prayers ~

Day

70

To God Be the Glory

Romans 15 v 25 – 16 v 27

Paul now draws this wonderful letter to a close in a way that is practical, prayerful, personal and praise-filled.

Practical

Read Romans 15 v 25-29

Having spoken of his mission (what we could call "spiritual help," v 15-22), Paul now turns to talk about giving "social help" to other Christians. It is a duty (something that is owed, v 27)—but it should also be joyful (we should be "pleased to do it," v 27).

How can this duty be done joyfully? By remembering that we have received spiritual blessings through the gospel, and so we please Christ by giving away material blessings (see 2 Corinthians 8 v 8-9). In this particular case, the Gentile churches were able to help materially those who had helped them spiritually—the Jerusalem churches from whom they'd heard the gospel (Romans 15 v 27).

Prayerful

Read Romans 15 v 30-33

How can the Roman church support Paul (v 30)?

Personal

Read Romans 16 v 1-24

What does Paul commend various people for in verses 1-16?

What do we learn about the life of the early church from this list?

Praise-Filled

Read Romans 16 v 25-27

What does Paul praise God for as he finishes his letter?

Why is it fitting that this particular letter ends with this kind of praise?

⊙ Apply

How are you, or how could you be:

• *helping other Christians practically?*

• *praying for those who are working for the gospel in dangerous places?*

• *living like the people Paul mentions in the Roman church? (You could pick a couple of descriptions that strike and challenge you.)*

• *praising God continually for your faith in the gospel of Christ?*

This is the end of our time in the book of Romans. Spend a few moments now reflecting on the book as a whole.

What has particularly excited you?

What has particularly challenged or changed you?

What questions or issues do you need to keep thinking about?

⊙ Pray

Praise and glorify God! You could use some verses from the letter that have especially resonated with you.

~ Notes and Prayers ~

_____

_____

_____

_____

_____

_____

_____

_____

_____

_____

_____

_____

_____

_____

_____

_____

_____

_____

_____

_____

_____

_____

_____

_____

How to
Face Trials

James 1 v 1-4

Welcome to the book of James. As we'll see, this is a book that shows us what genuine, wholehearted faith looks like in real life. It will challenge us and change us!

Meet James

Read James 1 v 1

Who is the letter from, and how does he describe himself?

How does he describe the recipients?

This James is also the younger brother of Jesus—but his self-introduction makes clear that far more important than that biological connection is the spiritual one he enjoys. More significant than being a younger brother of Jesus is being a servant of Jesus.

The "twelve tribes" is how the people of God were described in the Old Testament. He describes them as "scattered"—so this letter is to Jewish Christians, living outside Israel. But in a secondary sense, it is also to God's people who are scattered around the world throughout the generations—to us.

Pure Joy

Read James 1 v 2-4

What does James tell us to do (v 2)?

Why is this a very hard thing to do?

What reason for having this view of tough times does James give us in v 3-4?

How can we actually have this perspective? Notice James begins verse 2: "Consider." He tells us not so much how to feel as how to think. He is not saying, *Pretend this is fun.* He is telling us, *Remember what God is doing in this.* God will use trials to make us rounded Christians—to grow us into the very people we were created and saved to be. So trials are the spiritual equivalent of growbags—faith grows by learning to persevere in hardship (see Romans 5 v 3-4). Difficulties are opportunities to cling on to the promises of God more tightly.

So we are not to be joyful about suffering; but we are to be joyful in suffering, because we know what God can and does do for us through suffering.

⊘ Apply

Think of a trial you have recently gone through, or are going through right now.

Why did it (or does it) naturally take away joy from you? Why would it have been wonderful to be able to know "pure joy" in this?

Can you see any ways in which you were/are growing in perseverance, and becoming a more mature Christian through it?

How could you "consider" your trial in a way that makes you joyful, rather than joy-less?

⊙ Pray

None of this is easy, and we need God's help, as we'll see tomorrow (v 5). So pray that he would enable you to obey verse 2, either today or when a trial next arrives. And pray for Christian friends you know who are going through trials right now.

~ Notes and Prayers ~

_____

_____

_____

_____

_____

_____

_____

_____

_____

_____

_____

_____

_____

_____

_____

_____

_____

_____

_____

_____

Day

72

Wisdom in Confusion

James 1 v 5-8

Trials are an opportunity to grow—but that doesn't mean we'll instinctively be joyful in them, or know what to do about them. Trials and confusion tend to go together.

You Need to Ask

Read James 1 v 5

When we lack the ability to consider trials as pure joy, what should we do?

What happens when we do this?

To encourage us to ask God for wisdom, James gives us something wonderful—theology. He reminds us of what God is like:

• He is generous—he gives us wisdom whenever we ask for it.

• He gives to all—he gives wisdom to anyone who asks for it.

• He gives "without finding fault"—when we come to him in the middle of turmoil, he never says, *You really messed that up* or, *Don't you know by now how to handle this?*

These are central gospel truths—but in hard times, it is very easy to forget all of them.

How to Ask

Read James 1 v 6-8

What must we do, and not do, as we ask (v 6)?

How does verse 8 help us to understand what kind of person James is describing in verse 6?

So James is not saying: *If you have ever questioned or struggled or wrestled, don't expect God to give you anything.* He is saying: *If you come to God hedging your bets—asking for help while also looking elsewhere for help—then don't expect to find help from the Lord.*

In other words, we need to be as sincere about asking for God's wisdom as he is about giving it to us. But if we do come sincerely, then verse 5 is a promise made to us. We may pray for wisdom and still feel none the wiser—but we are promised that God's wisdom will direct us in the decisions we then go on to make. We may not feel any more confident, but God will protect us from folly.

⊘ Apply

Are you someone who tends to assume they'll make good decisions in a crisis? How do these verses challenge you?

Are you someone who tends to panic whenever faced with a big decision? How do these verses challenge you?

And how do these verses encourage and comfort you, whatever your temperament?

⊙ Pray

How are you finding it hard to consider trials "pure joy"?

How are you finding it hard to know how to act wisely?

Pray now that God would give you wisdom.

Pray that you would not hedge your bets, but ask sincerely.

And thank him that he promises that when you ask sincerely, he gives generously.

~ Notes and Prayers ~

Proud Christianity

James 1 v 9-12

N o one likes people who are proud of their position in life. The Bible says "God opposes the proud" (Proverbs 3 v 34). So what James says here is a little puzzling...

Read James 1 v 9-12

Humble Pride

How should poor Christians see themselves (v 9)?

Why are poor Christians in a "high position"? Because of the gospel, which means that however destitute you may be, you are a somebody. Spiritually, James is saying, you have it made. All that the Father has for his Son has been extended to those who are Christ's. Spiritually speaking, every Christian is a billionaire.

Humiliated Pride

How should rich Christians see themselves (v 10)?

What should they remember (v 10-11)?

How is this different from how the world tends to view wealth?

To become a Christian requires becoming "humiliated"—which is a very strong word! However rich someone is materially, they are utterly bankrupt spiritually—

---

their wealth will bloom and then wither, and their eternity depends entirely on God, not themselves.

There is something deceptive about wealth. It all too easily skews our view of ourselves and our abilities; and it's all too easy to become so used to being self-reliant that we cannot accept that for eternal life, we must be God-reliant. The rich man Jesus met walked away from the Savior not because he didn't want salvation, but because he couldn't bear to need it, nor to be parted from his wealth to have it (Mark 10 v 22).

But what matters is not whether we are poor or rich, a nobody or a somebody in the world, but whether we have come to Jesus for eternal life. The gospel lifts us and lowers us. And it promises us that in the future, we will enjoy unimaginable wealth...

Crown of Life

Re-read James 1 v 12

What does someone who keeps going in faith during trials receive (v 12)?

How are both poverty and wealth trials that we need to persevere through?

⊙ Apply

Is your view of yourself and your value shaped more by your status (economic, social, etc.) or by the gospel?

The poor need to reflect on the certainty of heaven; the rich, on the uncertainties of earth.

Which do you need to do? And what difference will grasping that perspective more firmly make to you today?

⊙ Pray

Read Proverbs 30 v 7-9 and make it a prayer.

~ Notes and Prayers ~

_____

_____

_____

_____

_____

_____

_____

_____

_____

_____

_____

_____

_____

_____

_____

_____

_____

_____

_____

_____

_____

_____

_____

_____

When Temted...

James 1 v 13-18

When we face trials, we tend to face temptations, too. So understanding temptation is vital if we are to respond rightly to difficult circumstances.

Help in Temptation

Read James 1 v 13-15

We are to expect temptation. James begins verse 13, "when," not "if." You are going to be tempted. The only question is whether you spot what is happening or not. We need to not be surprised by temptation, and we need to understand it.

What is NOT happening when we are tempted (v 13)?

What IS the cause of our temptation, does James say (v 14)?

Often, our reflex is to lay the blame for being tempted elsewhere, so we can excuse giving in to it. We might find ourselves thinking, *God made me like this. He's the one who gave me this weakness* or, *He's the one who put me in this situation.* But James exposes the uncomfortable truth that the evil desire tugging away at us is our own. We can't blame anyone else for our desire to sin.

If our evil desires are allowed to direct us, what does temptation lead to (v 15)?

How does this underline how important our response to temptation is?

⊙ Apply

Think about the last time you sinned.

How were you tempted? How did your evil desires entice you? How did this "give birth" to sin?

Have you accepted that this sin should lead to "death"? Have you asked for forgiveness?

Don't Be Deceived

Read James 1 v 16-18

James warns us not to "be deceived" (v 16), either about how bad we are, or about how good God is—which is what he now focuses on.

What does come from God (v 17)?

Notice that James reminds us that God is sovereign, dependable and gracious.

What is the best "good and perfect gift" we have been given (v 18)?

Our desires give birth to sin, which gives birth to death. But God has intervened. Through his word, he's given us a very different birth—into his new creation.

⊙ Pray

Thank God for the gifts he has given you today. Then thank him for giving you birth into new life.

Speak to God about ways in which you are being tempted to disobey him, especially if those temptations arise as a result of a trial you're facing. Pray that God would enable you to become "mature and complete," rather than you listening to and acting on your "evil desires."

~ Notes and Prayers ~

Are You Really Listening?

James 1 v 19-27

This passage poses the question, *Are you a good listener?* And then James shows us how to answer that question...

Slower, Faster

Read James 1 v 19-21

What should we be quick about, and slow about (v 19)? Why (v 20)?

Remember, James' first readers are Christians who are facing trials (v 2).

Why, when things are difficult, is it very easy to do the opposite of what James says in verse 19?

What do we need to get rid of, and what must we "accept" (v 21)?

We're called to change—and we're not going to change without God's word. Only when we learn to listen carefully to him can we begin to live lives that please him.

Like Looking in a Mirror

Read James 1 v 22-25

How is it possible to think we're listening to God's word, but actually not be truly listening at all (v 22-24)?

What is the proof that we are listening well (v 22, 25)?

When you look in a mirror, you act on what it shows you. And like a mirror, God's word shows us what we are really like. And we need to act on what it tells us about ourselves. We need to obey what it says.

Verse 25 gives us great motivation for "doing," not "forgetting," what we read in God's word. God's word is perfect. It is exactly what we need—we were designed to obey it. This is why we discover real freedom—the freedom of being ourselves—when we obey it, rather than when we choose our own way. As a fish is only truly free within the constraints of being in water, so a human is only truly free as they live within the constraints of God's law. Obedience should never be something we resent—every command God gives us is for our good.

We listen to God rightly when we not only hear his word, but accept it and then obey it.

Godly Religion

Read James 1 v 26-27

Verse 26 describes the kind of person who listens to God's word, but does not do what it says. The stark challenge is that not controlling our speech is a sign that we are not actually following God.

What sort of life is a sign that we are truly listening well to God's word (v 27)?

⊙ Apply

These verses are very challenging!

Can you see areas of your life where obeying God has led to blessing?

Do you know of areas where you are listening but not obeying? What will change? How will you use this passage to motivate you?

~ Notes and Prayers ~

_____

_____

_____

_____

_____

_____

_____

_____

_____

_____

_____

_____

_____

_____

_____

_____

_____

_____

_____

_____

_____

_____

_____

Day
76

No More
Favoritism

James 2 v 1-7

James has just told us that acceptable religion involves not "being polluted by the world" (1 v 27). Now he turns to giving us a concrete example of what that looks like.

Read James 2 v 1-7

Rich Man, Poor Man

What does James tell his "brothers and sisters" not to do (v 1)?

What scenario does he imagine (v 2)?

How is favoritism a rejection of the "religion that God our Father accepts," which James laid out in 1 v 27?

In Your Church?

We may think this would never happen in our church—and we might be right. But remember this scenario is just one example of "favoritism." The underlying attitude is that someone who is worth more in the world is worth more to the church. If this issue was a danger for Christians in James' day, we can be sure it's a danger in ours, too.

Can you think of scenarios in which this "favoritism" might show itself in your own church, or heart?

When we show favoritism in some way, what are we doing (v 4)?

How does this mean we are opposing the way that God works (v 5)?

Verse 5 is no less true today. Globally, the church is overwhelmingly poor. Many of the places where the gospel is advancing the fastest are poor. The pattern is hard to miss—God chooses to work by calling the world's poor to be spiritually rich.

This is not to say that God loves the rich less than the poor, or that the poor in some way deserve Christ's sacrifice. But it is to say that when we, in any way, treat those who are rich, or influential, or popular, or successful, better than those who are not, we are shunning the very people whom God chooses to bless.

We need to be careful about how we view those who are wealthy or privileged. I once worked for a church near a prestigious university. People would often say, "It's great you work there. These students are so strategic." But building a strategy around these "key people" contradicts James' words here. The privileged need saving because they are lost, not because they matter more or can contribute more. God's strategy, by and large, is to use "those who are poor in the eyes of the world" to achieve his purposes. After all, the wealthy and privileged often use their status to give Christians a hard time (v 6-7).

The church is not to resent the rich; but it is not to pin its hopes on them.

⊙ Apply

All of us are tempted toward favoritism.

What kind of favoritism are you in most danger of?

How does the gospel challenge that attitude?

Do you need to change how you think or act in any way?

~ Notes and Prayers ~

_____
_____
_____
_____
_____
_____
_____
_____
_____
_____
_____
_____
_____
_____
_____
_____
_____
_____
_____
_____
_____
_____

Day

77

Mercy Must Triumph

James 2 v 8-13

We've seen that favoritism of any kind contradicts God's choice. James now gives us two more reasons to fight that attitude: it also contradicts God's law and God's mercy.

Law

Read James 2 v 8-11

What law is broken when we show favoritism (v 8-9)? Why?

This is the "royal law" because it is the command that King Jesus put front and center (Mark 12 v 28-31). To love your neighbor means to love all your neighbors—and as soon as we think or act out of favoritism, we are breaking that command.

What does James say next about God's law (v 10)?

The law of God is one entity. The same Lawgiver stands behind all the commandments—we cannot excuse breaking one part of it because we are keeping all the other parts of it. That is like a murderer defending himself by saying: *I am a good husband, and have never committed adultery.* He is still a lawbreaker!

So how do these verses underline the seriousness of showing favoritism?

Mercy

Read James 2 v 12-13

What knowledge should our speech and actions reflect (v 12)?

What does verse 13 warn us of?

We should be people whose lives reflect God's standards. But more than this, how we show mercy to those around us reveals whether we truly know Jesus.

This isn't surprising—the very heart of why Jesus came was to show mercy. We demonstrate that we really know Jesus and have really received his mercy when we begin to show it to others. Mercy—loving those who do not deserve it, and cannot earn it—defines the gospel. This is why those who do not show mercy will not receive it (v 13)—because their lack of mercy shows they have never really grasped the gospel of mercy.

So if we are showing favoritism, James warns us not only that we are breaking God's law, but that we may not have understood God's gospel, either.

But James has already shown us what we must do when we are convicted by our favoritism...

Read James 2 v 1

We believe in a "glorious" Christ. His glory is not seen in great wealth and status, but on a criminal's cross. As we gaze at this, and only as we gaze at this, we cease to be impressed by worldly splendor; and we become merciful, and stop showing favoritism.

How does this challenge you?

⊙ Pray

Lord, let me be so captivated by your glory and so grateful for your mercy that I truly love my neighbors, I am truly compassionate to the needy, and I treat everyone as you treat me: with mercy. Amen.

~ Notes and Prayers ~

Day

78

How to Identify Fake Faith

James 2 14-19

"What good is it, my brothers and sisters, if someone claims to have faith but has no deeds? Can such faith save them?" (v 14). These questions should hit us hard.

James assumes a negative answer to both his questions. The genuinely frightening truth is that it is possible to claim and to believe that you possess genuine saving faith, when in fact you do not—to unknowingly have counterfeit faith.

So how can we tell if we possess true faith? James shows us what counterfeit faith is (which we'll see in this devotional) and what genuine faith looks like (which we'll see in the next one).

Just Sentimental?

Read James 2 v 14-17

What scenario does James imagine in verses 15-16?

What's the answer to his question at the end of verse 16?

What is a profession of faith without deeds a sign of (v 17)?

James isn't saying that faith is not real until it is acted on. He is saying that lack of actions reveal that faith is not real. You don't find out what someone truly believes by what they say, but by how they act. Real faith is not merely sentimental—wishing someone well while doing nothing to help them.

Just Doctrinal?

Read James 2 v 18-19

In verse 18, James imagines an objector saying, *There are different types of Christian. There are more "thinky," doctrinal types, and then there are more doing, practical types. You've got your faith; I've got my deeds.*

How does James underline that real faith is shown, though (end v 18)?

What belief is "good" (v 19)?

There is no truth more significant than this (see Deuteronomy 6 v 4; Mark 12 v 29).

And yet... who would wholeheartedly agree with this truth (James 2 v 19)?

Real faith is not about saying the right things. If we base our assurance on having our theology right, we need to remember that the demons have sound doctrine too.

James goes further: what the demons know to be true about God impacts them— they "shudder." Of course, true Christians will rejoice over who God is, and not shudder at it. But the question James is posing is: *does what you know about God actually matter to you?* Real faith is not merely doctrinal, or creedal—affirming something to be true which makes no difference to the way we live.

⊙ Apply

James is not asking us to look at other people's faith, but at our own.

How do these verses challenge you?

Remember, we will continue to think about this in the next study. For now, pray that God would show you if or where you need these verses to challenge and change you.

~ Notes and Prayers ~

How to Identify Real Faith

James 2 v 20-26

We've seen two types of counterfeit faith: sentimental non-acting "faith," and orthodox, non-impacting "faith." Now we'll see two real examples of genuine faith.

Abraham

Read James 2 v 20-24; Genesis 15 v 1-6; 22 v 1-19

What do we "see" in the Genesis 22 episode from Abraham's life (James 2 v 22, 24)?

Abraham's willingness to obey God proved that he really did trust God. His true, saving (or righteous-making) faith was seen in his obedience. The kind of faith that had been credited to Abraham years before in Genesis 15 now produced this act of incredible obedience in Genesis 22—the kind of act only a man of faith would perform. But...

Read Romans 3 v 28 and Ephesians 2 v 8-9

Is the Bible contradicting itself on this crucial question of how we are "righteous"— how we are saved? No—because the apostles are using the word "faith" differently. For Paul, faith equals trusting Christ—so we are saved by this alone, because it is the saving work of Christ alone that we trust. For James, as we've seen, faith equals claiming to trust Christ. Such "faith" is not, on its own, sufficient—saving faith involves both professing faith and living it out.

Furthermore, look again at the first two words of James 2 v 24. "You see..." James is talking not so much about how someone is saved, but how you see—how you can tell—that someone is saved. You could see Abraham was saved because of what he did. You can see that anyone is saved by what they do, not by their profession of faith—by what Paul himself called "the obedience that comes from faith" (Romans 1 v 5).

Rahab

Read James 2 v 25-26; Joshua 2 v 1-21

Rahab was in many ways very different to Abraham, but in one crucial aspect she was the same. She risked everything to align herself with the mission of Israel. Why? Because she had faith in Israel's God (Joshua 2 v 9-11). Because she believed in him, she acted for him. Her deeds showed that her faith was alive. Equally, a lack of deeds suggests a faith is actually dead (James 2 v 26).

⊙ Apply

How do you respond to this challenge as to whether your faith is fake or real?

Some of us think of our faults, and doubt that our faith is real. Others assume we're fine, without much proper reflection. It might be wise to ask a wise Christian who knows you well to give you their honest assessment of your "life of faith."

It may be that you are not a Christian, and your false faith has been exposed—in which case, thank God for showing you this, and ask him to give you true faith. But that may not be you—in which case, praise God for the true faith he has given you, despite all your flaws!

~ Notes and Prayers ~

_____

_____

_____

_____

_____

_____

_____

_____

_____

_____

_____

_____

_____

_____

_____

_____

_____

_____

_____

_____

The Power of Words

James 3 v 1-8

" **S** ticks and stones may break my bones, but words will never hurt me." It's a ditty often told to children. It is memorable. And it is inaccurate. Our words matter.

We're back to the theme James first raised in 1 v 26: "Those who consider themselves religious and yet do not keep a tight rein on their tongues deceive themselves..."

Teachers

Read James 3 v 1

What does James say about teachers in the church?

Why is this? Because teachers' words (whether from the pulpit, or in a children's group, or in any other setting) have the capacity to do particular damage to the church. Teachers either convey the truth, or they obscure it or even deny it.

⊙ Pray

Pray for those in your church who teach. Pray that they would speak truth clearly and lovingly, and never damage those in their care. If you have any kind of teaching role, pray that you would remember James 3 v 1 in your preparation and prayers.

Tongues

James 3 v 2-5a

In verse 2, "perfect" is the same word translated "complete" back in 1 v 4. Having control of your tongue is a sign of Christian maturity.

What else does it show that someone is able to do (end 3 v 2)?

How do the two visual aids in v 3-4 teach us about the power of our tongues?

⊘ Apply

Can you think of things you have said (or not said) that changed the course of your whole life, for better or for worse?

Untamed

Our tongues are powerful, for good or ill. And the problem, James says, is that generally our tongues are a force for the latter...

Read James 3 v 5b-8

What does the tongue tend to do (v 6)?

Notice where the "fire" comes from. Tongues are "set on fire by hell." Our unkind, destructive, malicious, lying words are hellish—they serve the purposes of the devil.

What are we incapable of doing (v 8)?

So James is not outlining a seven-step program to tongue-mastery. He is saying, *You desperately need to control your tongue, but you can't. It's beyond you.* Until we grasp this uncomfortable truth, we'll never truly seek the help of the One who can help—God.

⊙ Pray

Spend time reflecting on times recently when your tongue has been uncontrolled in some way. Don't excuse your words; confess them. And as you reflect on your failings, thank God for his forgiveness.

~ Notes and Prayers ~

Day
81

Taming the Tongue

James 3 v 9-18

J ames continues with his examination of our tongues. We've seen that they are powerful, destructive and uncontrollable. Now for a little more bad news, and then some help.

Revealing

Read James 3 v 9-12

What two things do we do with our tongues (v 9)?

Reflect on the last few days—how have you both praised God with your words, and been critical about or unkind toward people made in his image?

"This should not be" (v 10)—this two-faced speech is something no Christian should settle for. But often we don't even notice it.

What are the answers to James' questions in verses 11-12?

What point is he making?

James is, as so often, drawing on Jesus' own words during his time on earth (if you have time, *read Matthew 12 v 33-35*). The truth is that the product is always a reflection of the source. What our tongues say reveals what is going on inside us—what our hearts are really like. For most if not all of us, that is deeply challenging.

Help

We need help! At last, James offers some...

Read James 3 v 13-18

How can you tell if someone is truly wise (v 13)?

The opposite of a truly wise heart—which is seen in godly living, not clever words—is the heart of verse 14: one flourishing in "bitter envy and selfish ambition," directed by the devil, not God (v 15). And it is this kind of heart that drives a tongue that praises God but also tears down people made in his image.

What is different about godly wisdom, and how does it change someone's words and deeds (v 17-18)?

If we want to tame our tongues, we need to humble our hearts and seek wisdom from above. This wisdom means we'll speak and act in peace-filled ways (v 18). How do we get this kind of wisdom? By *reading James 1 v 5*—and then obeying it!

At Pentecost, the coming of the Spirit, seen in tongues of fire, caused the first disciples to use their words to declare Jesus' identity and offer his forgiveness (Acts 2 v 1-11). Our tongues can be set on fire by heaven, rather than by hell (James 3 v 6). If you are a Christian, this heavenly wisdom is your native tongue. You need to learn to be fluent in it. This is how you control your tongue—by seeking God's wisdom and help.

⊙ Apply

Think of a way in which your tongue is uncontrolled and destructive.

What does that reveal about your heart?

Will you ask for God's wisdom to change you?

What would be different about your words if they were directed by heaven?

~ Notes and Prayers ~

$$\frac{\textcircled{\substack{\text{Day} \\ 82}}}{}$$

Conflict Resolution

James 4 v 1-3

Conflict is part of everyday life, sadly. And it is often part of church life, equally sadly. But Christians can be different—and James shows us how.

Read James 4 v 1a (just the first sentence)

How would you answer the question?

Usually, we locate the problem firmly in someone else's court. What caused a quarrel with someone? *They did!* They were unreasonable, or demanding, or unhelpful...

The Real Problem

Read James 4 v 1-2

Where does James say fighting and quarreling come from (v 1)?

In other words, the issue is not everybody else... it is *me*. Conflict comes because our own selfish desires are not being met. We want and don't have—so we fight and we kill (v 2). James uses strong language, but as his older brother pointed out, we don't have to literally kill in order to commit a form of murder (read Matthew 5 v 21-22).

So to understand conflict, we need to understand the desire within us that is being frustrated. It might be the desire for a position of influence... or to get even... or to protect ourselves from criticism... or to have an easy, comfortable life.

What is the one thing James' readers don't do (end v 2)?

Prayerlessness is a sign that we are trying to run things in our own strength, for our own good, under our authority. *So often, James says, you don't have something because you didn't ask the one Person who can give it!*

But sometimes we do ask God, and yet we still don't get...

A Real Solution

Read James 4 v 3

Why don't we get what we ask for?

James is not talking about praying for a loved one to be healed, or an awful situation to be stopped. He is talking about praying "with wrong motives"—asking God merely to rubber-stamp our agenda. Our prayers should not be about getting God to do what we want, but about seeking to love to do what he wants.

So what causes conflict? It is the desires of our hearts. And what stops conflict? Praying, and doing so with more thought for God than ourselves. A humbly praying church will almost certainly not be a quarreling, divided church.

⊘ Apply

Think of a conflict you have been part of, in church or elsewhere.

What were the desires in you that caused and/or continued the conflict?

Did you pray? Did you pray with selfish motives? What happened next?

Is there an area of your life right now where you need to stop fighting, and start praying?

~ Notes and Prayers ~

Day
83

Always More Grace

James 4 v 4-6

O ur selfish hearts lead, as we've seen, to conflict with each other. But they also lead to a more serious conflict—one with God.

Don't You Know?

Read James 4 v 4

How do you respond to the first three words of this verse?

How does the rest of the verse explain what James means by "adulterous"?

Spiritually, you and I are unfaithful to God. The conflict between us that shows that we have selfish, worldly hearts is also a sign that we have adulterous hearts.

This marital language is not original to James; the Old Testament commonly speaks of God coming to his people as a husband comes to his bride, and of his people responding in unfaithfulness to him (e.g. Hosea 1 v 2; 2 v 1-13). Christians two-time God when we adopt the values and priorities of the world. And God takes it personally—just like a husband who finds his wife back in bed with the thug she was dating before he came into her life and rescued her from that awful relationship.

And being unfaithful to God provokes his enmity (end James 4 v 4).

⊘ Apply

Verse 4 shows us that the health of our relationship is quickly revealed by examining the desires in our hearts—are they godly or worldly? Do we chase the things the world chases, or are our deepest desires for the things of God—his reputation, the good of his people, and the service of others?

What do you see in your own heart?

But He Gives...

Read James 4 v 5-6

Verse 5 is hard to translate. It could be that by his Spirit God is jealous, or that he jealously longs for our "spirit"—our inner self—to be devoted to him. Either way, his concern and longing is that those who have wandered would return. He has not given up on us. He wants us back.

So what does he give us (v 6)?

What kind of attitude do we need to have toward him (v 6)?

Amazingly, each time we are unfaithful, God shows more undeserved, lavish kindness. But we cannot receive his grace if we are not willing to come back. We need to be humble about what we are like and what goes on in our hearts... to accept that we cannot be friends with the world and friends with God... and to come back. We need his grace. And wonderfully, he gives it.

⊙ Pray

Spend time asking God to enable you to see your own heart. Then confess ways in which you have been spiritually adulterous. And then thank God that he gives you more grace as you humbly return to him—and ask him to help you love him, and not the world.

~ Notes and Prayers ~

How to Return to God

James 4 v 7-12

J ames has called us to return humbly to God, to enjoy his grace, and to love him and not the world. Now he unpacks what that will look like.

The message of these verses is that there is grace for those who love and submit to God—but that the grace that forgives is also grace that changes and transforms people. In other words, receiving God's grace will prompt a change in behavior.

Our Dealings with God

Read James 4 v 7-10

How are we relate to God (v 7)? And to his enemy?

Submitting to God is part of what it means to relate rightly to him. He is not only or primarily your friend: he is your Creator and King. We are to submit our desires to him, asking him not to give us what we want if those things are selfishly motivated. This is easy to understand, but very hard to do. Our desires do not desire to be changed!

So even as we seek to submit to God, we must also resist the devil. He will tell us that our desires aren't bad; that they're natural; that working on them can be put off till later.

What is the wonderful promise at the end of verse 7?

The devil is not to be ignored or trivialized... but he is not to be overly feared, either. As we fight to submit to God, we put the devil to flight. As we turn back to God, we find him running to us to embrace us (v 7).

Verse 8 reminds us of what coming near to God involves. What is that?

Notice that repentance involves both hands and heart, actions and attitudes. And it also involves our emotions (v 9). James is not saying that there is no room for joy in the Christian life (remember 1 v 2). But there is, and must be, a place for real seriousness and grief about sin. The more we love Christ, the more we'll be grieved by our unfaithfulness. This is what it means to be humble—to be someone who God shows favor to (4 v 6), and lifts up (v 10).

Our Dealings with People

Read James 4 v 11-12

If we humble ourselves before God, what won't we do (v 11)?

Why? Because humbling ourselves before God reminds us that we are not him! We are not the judge; we are not the most important person; our efforts cannot save us.

⊙ Apply

Identify ways in which you have been "adulterous." Then move through verses 7-10, prayerfully. Submit... come near... wash... grieve... humble yourself. "And he will lift you up."

How will you do this daily from now on, and especially when you realize you have been caught in a sin?

~ Notes and Prayers ~

Day
85

Making
Plans

James 4 v 13-17

Next, James asks us the question: Who do you really think is in charge of your calendar?

Two Reminders

Read James 4 v 13-14

Who is James speaking to (v 13)?

This is all of us—we all need to make plans! But James wants us, as we make plans for today, tomorrow and next year, to remember two things.

What should we remember about the future (beginning of v 14)?

What should we remember about ourselves (end of v 14)?

We do not know whether we will finish reading this page before the Lord returns or we breathe our last. We are not in control of the next hour, let alone the next year. But since this thought is profoundly unsettling, we tend to avoid thinking it! We plan our lives as though we're in control; our default view is that once we plan something, it will happen. But it might not. We don't know.

Perhaps even more sobering, we are "a mist." The problem with making plans is that we can end up thinking that we are at the center of it all. But James says, *What is your life?* And then he gives us the title and strapline for our biography, summing up all our achievements and the product of all our plans...

Mist: Appeared for a while, and then vanished.

Our plans are not that significant!

James has thrown a cup of cold water in our faces... and he's done it so that we're able to listen to a different, better perspective...

A Right Perspective

Read James 4 v 15-17

What ought we to say as we make plans (v 15)?

This is not about sounding pious; it is about an attitude that recognizes that we don't know what will happen tomorrow, but God does; and that we are not at the center of everything, but God is. You are not the master of your destiny. But God is.

And this should affect not only how we plan, but what we plan. In v 13, the priority was profit. It is not wrong to make money—but it is wrong to have making money as the primary goal in our planning. Doing the Lord's will, for as long as it is his will for us to be around, is what is to inform our plans.

So this is why James calls the planning of verse 13 boastful, even "evil" (v 16). It's an arrogant view of the future, and of self—and it's a view that's forgetful of God's sovereignty.

⊙ Apply

When you make plans, do you do so as a Christian, or as if you're an atheist?

What plans are you currently making? Are you making sure you remember that they will only happen if they are the Lord's will—and that they need to be directed by the Lord's will?

~ Notes and Prayers ~

How to See the Wealthy

James 5 v 1-6

We've already seen that James doesn't hold back in his words and imagery! And this passage contains some of the strongest language anywhere in the New Testament.

Read James 5 v 1-6

Target Audience

Who needs to listen, and what should they be doing (v 1)?

There are good reasons to think James isn't addressing rich Christians (as in 1 v 10-11), but rather rich non-Christians. James often addresses people as "brothers and sisters" but not here. And there is talk of judgment, but none of salvation.

But why would James speak to those who won't be listening as his letter is read out in the churches? Because his purpose here is not so much to teach the ungodly rich about the error of their ways, but to show his Christian readers on the receiving end of their ungodliness (5 v 4, 6—see 2 v 6-7) what God thinks of it. He wants his readers to know how to think of the rich people around them—neither to envy them, nor to aspire to be like them, nor to grow bitter that they are not like them.

Do you recognize envy, aspiration and/or bitterness within yourself as you think of those you know who are not Christians, and who are wealthier than you?

It's What You Do with It

Why should the ungodly rich "weep and wail" (v 1)?

What's happening to their stuff (v 2-3)?

The point James is making is that these people have gathered wealth for its own sake. They have bought stuff so that they have stuff. And it won't last. Wealth is to be used, James is saying, not amassed.

What time are we living in (end v 3)?

James means the period before Christ's return, the judgment and the new creation.

Why does this make trusting in riches foolish?

What have these rich people used their money for (v 5)?

Wealth is to be used in the service of others, James is saying, and not amassed for selfish pleasures. To be selfish in your pursuit and use of wealth is to live like a turkey eating everything in sight in late November, unaware that the day of slaughter is coming.

How have these rich people treated others (v 4)?

Most of us in the West are rich, relatively—so how does v 4 challenge us?

⊙ Apply

How do these verses teach you to view those around you who are not Christians, and are wealthier than you?

Does verse 4 prompt you to change where you shop and/or how you treat those who provide services or work for you?

Should these verses change how you pray for yourself or others in any way?

~ Notes and Prayers ~

How to
Wait Well

James 5 v 7-12

J ames now turns his attention from rich to poor, from non-Christian to
Christian, and from oppressors to oppressed. His counsel is, as usual,
direct, pithy and practical.

Have Patience

Read James 5 v 7-9

What does James tell his "brothers and sisters" to be (v 7)?

Remember, these believers were the objects of oppression and violence (v 4, 6).
James calls for patience, not revolution. Why? Because of what their faith tells them
is true, even in times of persecution.

What has he already reminded his readers of (end v 3, end v 4, end v 5)?

What does he promise them now (v 8)?

Despite appearances, God does care, and God will act. Justice will be done. Knowing
this enables James' readers to be patient and stand firm in their faith. They are to
be like a godly farmer (v 7), who patiently waits for the rain that God kindly sends
(Deuteronomy 11 v 13-14), trusting that it will come.

What are his readers not to do, as they face oppression (v 9)?

When we face difficulty and injustice, it's very easy to turn against each other—to be bitter that other Christians have it easier, or to grow annoyed with other Christians not responding to their own trials as well as we think they should. *Don't!* says James.

Exemplary Patience

Read James 5 v 10-12

Which two examples of "patience in the face of suffering" does James give (v 10-11)?

The suffering of God's prophets reminds us that suffering is not novel; and that it is not impossible to remain faithful and fruitful in hard times. Suffering and being "blessed" (v 11) are not incompatible. That's what the suffering of Job underlines— he lost everything, he refused to curse God, and God blessed him.

What are James' readers not to do, as they face suffering (v 12)?

As in verse 9, James shows that our tongues can ruin everything. Waiting with patience means speaking with patience, and not making unrealistic vows or being people whose word is usually unreliable, and who therefore need to make an oath in order to be trusted. God condemns us (not in an eternal sense, but in the sense of showing his displeasure) when we exaggerate, speak half-truths, or fail to keep our word.

⊙ Apply

How does remembering Jesus is on the way, and will bring justice and restoration, change your view of the hard parts of your life right now?

How and when are you tempted to grumble about others, or to fail to keep your word? How will you speak positively and be trustworthy instead?

~ Notes and Prayers ~

Day
88

Whatever is Happening...

James 5 v 13-18

The last part of James 5 is very hard to understand. We'll take three days to look at it—and as with any difficult text, it helps to rule out first what it can't mean.

Read James 5 v 13-18

What James Isn't Saying

Though confusing, this is clear enough for us to know that James *isn't* talking about:

- *the Roman Catholic practice of "last rites,"* where someone on their deathbed is anointed with oil by a priest, confesses, and is therefore (spiritually) saved. But here, James suggests the sick person will not die, but actually recover (v 15).

- *healing rallies, or particular people having healing ministries.* These verses suggest something happening in a home, not at a rally (v 14). The "call," or invitation, is from the sick people to the elders, not the other way around (v 14). And those doing the praying are run-of-the-mill elders, not a specially gifted "healer."

- *an unbreakable link between believing prayer and certain healing.* We see many examples in the Bible of godly, sick people *not* being miraculously healed. Timothy is told to drink wine for his stomach problems, not to pray harder (1 Timothy 5 v 23). This is crucial, because Christians of good faith and conscience can be crushed by claims that if they'd only exercised enough faith or offered enough prayer, then they or a loved one would have been healed.

- *merely spiritual healing, with no physical aspect.* If James had not wanted to talk about physical healing, surely he would not have spoken in terms that naturally lead us to think about physical healing!

What James Is Saying

So what *is* James saying?!

What should we do when in trouble (v 13a)?

What should we do when happy (v 13b)?

What should we do when ill (v 14)?

So first, the headline here is: *Whatever is happening, prayer is the right response.*

Second, the whole letter is about living with genuine, wholehearted faith, and returning to that life when we wander from it. In these verses, James seems to identify sickness with sin (v 15 is literally "The prayer offered ... will make the sick person saved"), and healing with repentance (v 16). Sickness is not always or usually the result of sin (e.g. John 9 v 1-3)—but it can be (1 Corinthians 11 v 28-30). So in a context of Christians struggling with half-heartedness, James says, *If you are sick, call for the elders, because you may (not must) be experiencing God's disciplines, and that's a spiritual matter for which you need spiritual help.*

And it is not only the elders who are part of this ministry of spiritual restoration (and, in some cases, physical healing). It is "each other" (James 5 v 16). Repentance is a church family concern.

⊙ Apply

Are you someone to whom others would feel able to confess sins without being condemned, belittled or excused?

Are you someone who is willing to confess your sins to others and ask for prayer and help?

~ Notes and Prayers ~

Day
89

Prayers That Change Things

James 5 v 16-18

If in trouble—pray (v 13). If sick—pray (v 14). If sinful—pray (v 16). But does prayer actually work? Does it really change anything?

The Claim

Read James 5 v 16

What does James claim here?

If we are walking in the grace of God, seeking to live wholehearted lives of genuine faith, then we have the opportunity to make a huge difference in the lives of others, because our prayers change things. But... really?!

The Real-Life Evidence

Read James 5 v 17-18

Who is the real-life example James points us to (v 17)?

What does he tell us about him (v 17a)?

In many ways, Elijah was *not* just like us—God chose him as his prophet, and performed spectacular miracles through him. But James is focusing not on Elijah's miracles, but Elijah's *prayers*. When it comes to praying, he *is* just like we are (or can be)—a wholehearted, though flawed, "righteous" follower of God.

Scan-read 1 Kings 17 – 18

What did Elijah's prayers achieve (James 5 v 17b)?

What did his prayers do next (v 18)?

How powerful were his prayers?!

When we find ourselves praying as a gesture, but not really expecting anything to happen, we need to remember Elijah: his prayers changed the weather, for years! How foolish we are not to pray far more than we do, and for more than we do.

And James is also making a deeper point. Elijah didn't pray for arbitrary or self-serving things. By praying for drought in a time of rampant spiritual adultery, Elijah was praying for judgment on sin that would wake the people up to what they were doing. He wanted to challenge the people to stop wavering between two opinions (1 Kings 18 v 21), to stop being double-minded—just as James does! When the people chose to worship God, not idols, Elijah then prayed for rain—for God's restoration and blessing.

So Elijah teaches us that the prayers that are powerful and effective are the prayers that a "righteous" person wants to pray—prayers for the honor of God's name, for the wholeheartedness of his people, and for the salvation of more people.

It is a wonderful privilege to pray according to God's purposes as they become our own desires, and then to watch our prayers change things as God responds to our prayers.

⊘ Pray

How will these two verses change:

• *how you feel about praying?*

• *how often you pray?*

• *what you pray about?*

If you trust in and seek to follow Christ, you are righteous! So, as a righteous person, pray now—it's powerful and effective!

~ Notes and Prayers ~

Day

90

Search and Rescue

James 5 v 19-20

J ames has spent his letter exhorting us to return to or sustain wholehearted, genuine faith. As he closes, he sends all of us out on a spiritual search-and-rescue mission.

Bring Them Back

Read James 5 v 19-20

What scenario is pictured in verse 19?

What truths are given that motivate us to "bring that person back" (v 19)?

My brother's or sister's struggle isn't just their problem—it is mine. We need to be willing to urge the struggling, wayward Christian to come back to wholehearted faith.

Trying to "bring that person back" is not easy. It risks losing their friendship or their respect. And in many cultures (perhaps especially British culture), we've been taught to mind our own business and to avoid conflict. But God doesn't call us to be British; he calls us to be Christian. And that means appreciating that wandering from the faith leads to death (v 20)—and therefore determining to do all we can to bring the wanderer back to faith, so that the Lord Jesus will cover over all their sins, as he has ours.

James isn't calling us to do anything he won't do himself. This letter, in many ways, is a search-and-rescue mission, asking us whether our faith may be counterfeit, challenging us about how we may not be living wholeheartedly, and showing us what a life of genuine faith looks like. We are to do the same for our "brothers and sisters" (v 19).

Read Galatians 6 v 1

What commands and help does Paul give us "if someone is caught in a sin"?

⊙ Apply

What would stop you seeking to bring someone back from wandering?

Is there anyone with whom, right now, the Spirit is prodding you to have a difficult conversation (perhaps about ungodly relationships, or priorities)? Will you talk to them?

The End of James

James is a book full of challenge, but equally full of the promise that living wholeheartedly for our "glorious Jesus Christ" (2 v 1) will lead to patience and blessing in suffering (5 v 7-8, 11), joy in trials (1 v 2), and, in the end, the crown of life (1 v 12).

As we finish, scan-read through the whole letter, thinking about:

• *what has particularly challenged you.*

• *what has particularly encouraged you.*

• *what you need to think more about.*

• *what changes you need to make to your attitudes or actions.*

⊙ Pray

Turn your answers into prayers for yourself and your church, remembering that "the prayer of a righteous person is powerful and effective" (5 v 16).

~ Notes and Prayers ~

EXPLORE
BY THE BOOK

More from the Series...

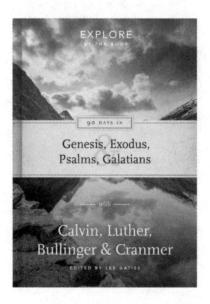

L et four of the great Bible teachers of the Reformation—
John Calvin, Martin Luther, Heinrich Bullinger and Thomas
Cranmer—teach you the Scriptures, day by day. Edited by Lee
Gatiss, this devotional brings the work of these sixteenth-century
giants to life in an engaging and accessible way.

> *Makes some of the most spiritually penetrating devotional
> writing of the past accessible to readers today. Don't miss it!*

Tim Keller

> *Imagine bringing the great Reformers to your house for personal
> devotions. This book comes closest to that.*

Michael Horton

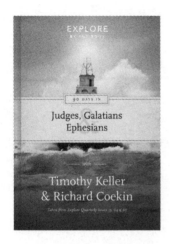

Tim Keller, along with Richard Coekin, Director of the Co-Mission church-planting network in London, UK, take you through the gripping days of the Judges, the gospel freedom of Galatians, and the Christ-centered glories of Ephesians.

Join Mark Dever, Senior Pastor of Capitol Hill Baptist Church, Washington DC, and Mike McKinley, Senior Pastor of Sterling Park Baptist Church, Virginia. They will take you through the twists and turns of the life of Ruth, the searing challenges and soaring promises of Jeremiah, and the local-church exhortations of Paul's first letter to the Corinthian church.

the**good**book
COMPANY

www.thegoodbook.com/explorebythebook

EXPLORE

DAILY DEVOTIONAL

Meet the rest of the Explore family. *Explore Quarterly* is a numbered, dated resource that works through the entire Bible every seven years in quarterly publications and features contributions from trusted Bible teachers such as Tim Keller, Mark Dever, Al Mohler, Richard Coekin, and H.B. Charles Jr. The *Explore App* brings open-Bible devotionals to your smartphone or tablet, enabling you to choose between dated studies, studies on a specific book, and topical sets.

www.thegoodbook.com/explore

thegoodbook
COMPANY
Opening up the Bible

At The Good Book Company, we are dedicated to helping Christians and local churches grow. We believe that God's growth process always starts with hearing clearly what he has said to us through his timeless word—the Bible.

Ever since we opened our doors in 1991, we have been striving to produce resources that honor God in the way the Bible is used. We have grown to become an international provider of user-friendly resources to the Christian community, with believers of all backgrounds and denominations using our Bible studies, books, evangelistic resources, DVD-based courses and training events.

We want to equip ordinary Christians to live for Christ day by day, and churches to grow in their knowledge of God, their love for one another, and the effectiveness of their outreach.

Call us for a discussion of your needs or visit one of our local websites for more information on the resources and services we provide.

Your friends at The Good Book Company

NORTH AMERICA thegoodbook.com 866 244 2165
UK & EUROPE   thegoodbook.co.uk   0333 123 0880
AUSTRALIA   thegoodbook.com.au   (02) 6100 4211
NEW ZEALAND   thegoodbook.co.nz   (+64) 3 343 2463

 WWW.CHRISTIANITYEXPLORED.ORG
Our partner site is a great place for those exploring the Christian faith, with a clear explanation of the good news, powerful testimonies and answers to difficult questions.